Little Shoes

Little Shoes

The Sensational Depression-Era Murders That

Became My Family's Secret

Pamela Everett

Skyhorse Publishing

Skyhorse Publishing books may be purchased in bulk at special discounts for sales promotion, corporate gifts, fund-raising, or educational purposes. Special editions can also be created to specifications. For details, contact the Special Sales Department, Skyhorse Publishing, 307 West 36th Street, 11th Floor, New York, NY 10018 or info@skyhorsepublishing.com.

Skyhorse® and Skyhorse Publishing® are registered trademarks of Skyhorse Publishing, Inc.®, a Delaware corporation.

Visit our website at www.skyhorsepublishing.com.

10 9 8 7 6 5 4 3 2 1

Library of Congress Cataloging-in-Publication Data is available on file.

Cover design by Brian Peterson

Print ISBN: 978-1-5107-3130-1
Ebook ISBN: 978-1-5107-3131-8

Printed in the United States of America

For my aunts
Marie and Madeline.
Forever in my heart.

CONTENTS

PROLOGUE

Reno, Nevada
Summer, 1978

I WAS FIFTEEN years old when I did what countless teenage girls had done before me. I lied and said I was spending the night with a friend and instead, I went to my boyfriend's house.

My dad found out and showed up at the boyfriend's front door. When I saw him standing there, it was like time stopped. He had to be furious.

But he wasn't angry. It was strange, almost like he was sad and a little shaken. I was fine and my boyfriend and I were just watching TV, but it was as if my dad was seeing something else, some scene visible only to him. He said he was there to take me home. We drove the entire way in silence. I wanted to die.

Back home, he sat me down at the kitchen table. I noticed he was trembling a little. I'd never seen him like that. He turned to ritual to steady himself, lighting a cigarette and dangling it from the corner of his mouth as he flipped shut the metal top on his old lighter and methodically put it back in his pants pocket. He positioned the ashtray just so, took a quick drag, and set the cigarette in its slot, tip up so it would burn evenly. I'd seen it a million times.

Then he started in a low, quiet voice. His sentences were short and measured.

"You can't lie to me. You can't tell me you're one place and go somewhere else. You can't ever make me search for you like I did tonight."

He'd barely finished when I erupted with teen outrage that he was making a federal case—one of his favorite phrases—out of nothing. I cried, "You never let me do anything! My friends get to do so many things I can never do. I have to be home so early and I can't go anywhere. I just wanted to get out of the house for once! Why won't you *ever* let me do anything?!"

He didn't look at me. He picked up his cigarette and tapped it lightly against the ashtray. He was taking careful breaths, looking down, watching the smoke curl up from the table. The silence seemed to go on forever. I was so angry.

And then I realized that he was trying not to cry.

When parents divorce and a teenage girl stays with her dad, father and daughter will experience countless awkward moments. But this was unimaginable, watching my big bear of a dad choking back tears. He was insanely strict and we didn't always get along, but I loved him, and since the divorce, we'd grown very close. In the first months after my mom moved out, I felt like he was all I had. He felt that way, too. I'll never forget seeing him like that, and I'll never forget what he said next.

"I lost two sisters and I can't lose my daughter."

He was really fighting the tears now. Oh God, I felt so ashamed for causing all this. I dropped my defenses and tried to think of something, anything to say.

"What, Dad?"

"They found them—they found their pairs of little shoes lined up in a row."

And then he broke down.

"Dad?"

Before I could go to him or ask another question, he shook his head, gathered himself, and went to his bedroom. He closed the door behind him and I knew he couldn't talk about it, whatever it was, anymore or probably ever. And I would never be courageous enough to ask him. Instead, I asked my mom about it a few weeks later by phone. She hesitated, but finally said yes, he lost—there was that word again—two sisters but he's never been able to talk about it. She knew very little, just the basics. She told me to leave it alone. I did.

My dad died ten years later having never mentioned his sisters or those little shoes again. But I never forgot that night at the kitchen table and many years later I finally started digging. I had to go back in time nearly eighty years, into another world and a crime that changed my family forever. I'm an attorney and a criminal justice professor, and before my legal career, I was a broadcast journalist who covered the crime and criminal court beat. I drew on those experiences to slip back into police headquarters, the courtrooms, and the press conferences of the day and piece together the events of the summer of 1937.

I also had to get back inside a little house in Inglewood, California, and into the hearts and minds of the people who lived through those terrible events, to maybe understand how they endured.

And most difficult, I had to get to know the accused killer—his life, his alleged crime, his ride through the criminal justice system, and his execution.

What I found amazed me. A notorious triple murder case that made news from coast to coast; a case that challenged law enforcement while bringing them together in an unprecedented cooperation of effort; a case that led to one of the earliest recorded criminal profiles and to the first sex offender registration law that became the model for such laws in most states today; a case that—at least through my eyes as a volunteer for the California Innocence Project—raises serious questions about whether the State of California convicted and executed the wrong man.

And finally, I found a hidden and defining chapter in my family's history with details about a grandfather I never met, secrets in the heart of a grandmother I thought I knew, the lost childhoods of aunts and uncles, and the impact on a father whose life was forever changed and who then changed mine.

This is my story.

This is my family's story.

THE PARK

Centinela Park—Inglewood, California
Saturday, June 26, 1937

ALL THE NEWSPAPER stories begin the same, in the same place, with a scene that's unthinkable today. Three little girls playing alone in a park in Los Angeles. The two sisters—my aunts Melba Marie and Madeline Everett—were just nine and seven years old. Their playmate Jeanette Stephens was eight. They were all wearing summer dresses. I still cringe every time I think about them there.

But it was 1937, a seemingly simpler and safer time, and the park was filled with people. The school year had ended only a few weeks earlier and the summer was fresh and new, stretching out forever in everyone's minds. Kids were everywhere, at the baseball diamond, the popcorn stand, the picnic areas, and the community pool that sparkled aqua blue in the California sunshine. Centinela Park was a beautiful centerpiece of people and scenery in the quiet little bedroom community of Inglewood.

The park was also an oasis of inexpensive entertainment and escape during those hungry Depression-era years. Los Angeles County was especially hard hit—the worst in the state. Some seventy thousand people came pouring into Southern California just that year, most of them from the hopeless dust bowl areas and all of them desperately looking for work. California was the promised land. And a little town like Inglewood with a park like Centinela, its lush lawn and trees, its pool and picnic tables, was almost dreamlike. That Saturday morning in late June was one of those especially magical days.

1

The three girls walked to the park mid-morning. The Everett and Stephens families lived just a few doors down from each other on a street just across from the park. Melba Marie Everett and her little sister, Madeline, brought the old army blanket from home and spread it out under a pepper tree that fanned like a huge umbrella over their favorite spot. They also brought toys and a thermos of milk. Their older sister, eleven-year-old Olive Everett, said she'd be over later to meet them. Yes, I'll see you at "our tree." Under the pepper tree was her favorite spot, too. They were all fixtures there, just about every day since summer vacation started.

Another friend, ten-year-old June Hazley, came a short time later to play, and so did seven-year-old Theresa Zeigler, who joined them running in and out of a big drainage pipe, playing in the little stream that emptied from the pipe into the grassy area near their picnic blanket. Lillian Popp and her cousin Amy Lancey wandered over, too. But the other girls eventually left and the original trio stayed and played on their own. At the time, no one thought twice about any of it.

About eleven o'clock, Jeanette ran to the swimming pool attendant, Miss Wann, and asked for a piece of rope. Jeanette said, "Eddie, you know, Eddie the Sailor, wants to show us some rope tricks. He can do all kinds of tricks. He's been showing us some card tricks and now he wants a rope!" Miss Wann smiled and nodded to a nearby worker, who gave the little girl some rope. Jeanette squealed "thank you!" and hurried back to the picnic blanket.

About forty-five minutes later, fifteen-year-old Dorothy Reitz was sunning near the pool when she noticed a man sitting off to her side. He was watching the children in the pool. A few moments later, he was walking around the pool holding a little girl's hand. The girl had such beautiful blond hair, Dorothy noticed. The man leaned down and whispered something to the little girl and she laughed as she scurried away past the popcorn stand.

AT NOON, THE three girls skipped up to the checkstand near the swimming pool. Marie asked Mr. Flynn, the attendant, "Will you take care of these things for us for a little while?" and she handed him the neatly folded blanket and a shopping bag that held a teddy bear and a few other playthings. Flynn checked the items and the girls scampered off. Little Madeline clutched a Mickey Mouse book she just couldn't part with, and Marie took the thermos of milk.

Mrs. Craycroft, the swimming pool matron, was coming across the big open grass area outside the pool when she saw the girls racing by. She knew them all, had seen them playing in the park so many times before.

"My, my, girls, why all the hurry?" she asked as they ran by.

"We're going to hunt rabbits! We're going to hunt rabbits!" the girls answered in an excited chorus. "Going to hunt rabbits!" they sang as they danced away to where the park opened out onto Warren Lane, in the direction of the Baldwin Hills.

BACK HOME, OLIVE was working. She really wanted to get over to the park to play, but she was trying to do as many chores as possible to help her mom and dad. They assigned chores to all the children, except the littlest ones, and they'd all pitched in that morning. But Olive felt bad that her parents were always working so much, and she didn't want them to have to work more on the weekend. No, she would stay and do a few more chores.

LATE SATURDAY AFTERNOON, Vernon Aguilla, a Standard Oil employee, saw smoke rising from the Baldwin Hills. Standard Oil operated oil derricks in and around the hills, and he worried that an out-of-control campfire could threaten the nearby oil fields. He went to investigate and as he reached the end of a dirt road, he saw a man come down out of the hills near a ravine. The man said nothing and hopped into a 1929 or 1930 Ford roadster. Vernon remembered that the car didn't have any fenders but it did have a box on the back.

Joseph Fields was a chauffeur for a Works Progress Administration executive. He was driving that evening about 5:30 when he saw a WPA school crossing guard walking from the direction of the Baldwin Hills. He thought it was funny that a crossing guard would be there at the busy intersection of Slauson and La Brea Avenue, so far from a school and so late on a Saturday.

Mrs. Margaret Rigby was at her home on North Commercial Avenue, on the direct route between Centinela Park and the Baldwin Hills, when she saw a man run by with what looked like blood on his clothes. She thought it was around 5:30.

ABOUT THE SAME time, my grandparents, Melba and Merle Everett, were beginning to wonder why Marie and Madeline hadn't arrived home for dinner and their favorite radio programs. The Stephens parents were similarly keeping an eye out for Jeanette. It wasn't like any of the girls to be late. Eventually, my grandparents sent Olive, and Mrs. Stephens sent her son, Garth, to look for the girls over at the park.

But Garth didn't find them, and neither did Olive. She went to their spot under the pepper tree, and then by the pool, the popcorn stand, and even farther down by the baseball diamonds, but she didn't see them anywhere.

At 6:30, when the parents' worry must have been morphing into panic, my grandfather called the Inglewood Police Department to report the girls missing.

But it was too late. The nightmare had begun.

THE SEARCH

Inglewood, California
June 26–27, 1937

THE INGLEWOOD POLICE officer who took my grandfather's call that night assured the anxious father that everything would be fine. Standard police practice in those days was to wait at least twenty-four hours before filing a missing persons report, officers having gone on too many wild-goose chases for kids who turned up later at a friend's house or who returned home ashamed and sorry for a hasty attempt at running away.

The Everett and Stephens parents checked in with each other several times during the next hour or so, but there were still no signs of their girls. They tried to believe what the police officer told Mr. Everett, but when they talked about having to wait through the night, even one more hour was too long. At 8:30, after it was completely dark, Mr. Everett and Mrs. Stephens went down to the police station while Mr. Stephens searched the park again.

Merle Everett explained to the front desk officer that it simply wasn't possible the girls had run away. They'd been at the park that day, where they loved to play. The only place they would go other than the park was home, and all three were missing. They were little girls; Madeline was just seven years old. They weren't adventurous boys who might go exploring all day and into the night. *Please, it's getting so late.*

The officer excused himself and talked with the captain on duty. He told Captain Muir that this one sounded a little different. Maybe they should take a look.

The radio call went out to officers on patrol about 8:45. They kept an eye out for more than an hour, talked to people around town, but found nothing, which was odd because people always noticed kids who were out late, kids who seemed like they might be lost. It would be especially hard to miss three little girls.

About 10:00, Captain Muir called Inglewood Police Chief Oscar Campbell at home. When Campbell heard the story, he shuddered and told Muir to get the report out on radio and teletype so the LA Police Department and County Sheriff's Department would be on alert. He also told Muir to get Detective Joe Long and his men out there to look for park attendants or anyone who might have seen the girls earlier that day. Within no time, police learned from the swimming pool attendant about the rabbit hunt. A man had asked little Jeanette to get some rope. He was holding her hand later. They all went running by so fast.

Around 11:00, with no sign of the girls, Chief Campbell asked Mr. Everett and Mr. Stephens to come in to file a missing persons report. He also ordered every Inglewood police officer into the station.

Within hours, hundreds of searchers—Inglewood and Los Angeles police officers, sheriff's deputies, Legionnaires, Boy Scouts, and citizen posses—were on the ground, the city lit by an almost full moon. They scoured vacant houses, sheds, and weed patches and every other conceivable place where the girls might be. They worked tirelessly through the night until dawn.

But they found nothing. No one. Not a trace. And every hour that passed made it less likely they would find anything, ever.

At daybreak, Chief Campbell issued a statewide alert for the missing girls. He also personally called his counterparts in all the nearby beach cities—Santa Monica and Hermosa, Redondo, and Manhattan Beaches.

Barely stopping for rest or food, the teams were back in action early Sunday morning. Chief Campbell told the men the little girls' parents were of modest means, so kidnapping was out of the question. Dreading what he already knew must be true, he ordered officers to bring in every "known degenerate" in the community, question them, and tell them to stay put indefinitely where police could find them.

Searchers fanned out to the Baldwin Hills, just northwest above Slauson and South La Brea, where the bodies of the little Martin sisters had been found back in 1924. The killer, S. C. Stone—who'd escaped the noose and got life in prison with a last-minute reprieve from the governor—hid their bodies in a ravine under heavy brush and searchers didn't find them for nearly six months. Chief Campbell remembered that case all too well.

By mid-morning Sunday, more than five hundred people were part of a mass effort, including forty members of the Santa Monica Mounted Police, who were invaluable in the Baldwin Hills' rugged terrain. Search planes from the Sheriff's Department droned overhead. Even private pilots from the local Burdette airport and the Inglewood Aero Squadron took to the skies searching for the children.

Also by mid-morning, the news was all over Inglewood. Mothers made up reasons to keep their children indoors. Theresa Zeigler's mom held her especially close. Theresa had played with those girls in the park that very morning just before they disappeared. Telephone lines burned and adults gathered on front porches to compare notes. Centinela Park was so quiet compared to most summer Sundays, with only occasional curious onlookers wandering near the grassy area by the pool where the girls were last seen under their favorite pepper tree.

THESE EARLY HOURS were an impressive display of manpower and cooperation, with three agencies working together. The Inglewood Police Department, the LAPD, and the Sheriff's Department pooled officers and other resources. Fights over turf and territory could have seriously weakened the investigation, or Inglewood officers might have opted to handle the early stages on their own, until they were more certain about the scope of the case. But Inglewood Chief Campbell knew this case was bigger than his department, indeed possibly bigger than the state of California.

THE *LOS ANGELES* *Times* reported that the two fathers, my grandfather and Floyd Stephens, were on the ground, searching desperately for their girls. I could not imagine.

But I could imagine my dad and his best friends Ernie Klapproth and Cal Hazley looking everywhere, courageously breaking trail in the dense brush of the Baldwin Hills, as Ernie recounted it to his family many years later. He said my dad had to stop several times, confessing how he wanted to find his little sisters but at the same time praying with every step that he wouldn't.

Even before I heard that story, I'd always assumed my dad was part of the search. After he found out his sisters were missing and that he hadn't been there to prevent it from happening, that someone had so ferociously violated his family, he would have worked double time to right his wrong, to atone for the sin of not saving them when they needed him most. He would have been agonized and the only way he could have endured it in those early days was to search and search and search. He was only thirteen years old, but he would have been there.

But the newspaper reports never mention him. I can't find him in any of the photographs.

THE EVERETTS

Boston, Massachusetts
August 1934

MY GRANDPARENTS DECIDED in 1934 to move their family across the country from Boston to California. I always see them sitting at the kitchen table, probably early in the morning before the children were up for school, or maybe one night after the little ones were in bed, finally alone so they could discuss their plans. I never knew my grandfather, but a family friend described him as the "quintessential New England patriarch," so I'm certain he didn't discuss "things" in the presence of his children and instead, set the proper time and place for everything.

Another friend told me that my grandparents and their home were decidedly "Bostonian," so I see them drinking tea from fine china cups and an heirloom teapot, with a spoon tray and sugar cubes arranged just so on a tiny plate between them, the fabric tablecloth with lace edges that my grandmother made herself. She practiced the lost art of lace-making—known as "tatting"—and I could watch her for hours, mesmerized by the rhythmic way she moved the shuttle and worked the thread, giving me occasional glimpses of her creation as it grew magically behind her busy hands. Perhaps she was even tatting while they talked, shuttling a little nervously as they planned their move and a new life in the West.

The move would be a major undertaking, and not just because of the distance. They had six children, three boys and three girls. Their oldest was my dad, named after his grandfather, Perley Mandell

Everett, then their oldest daughter, Olive, then another son, Merle, who went by "Junior." Merle was a twin but the other son, Charles, died in childbirth. Then came the little girls, Melba Marie and Madeline Phyllis, and finally their youngest, Carl. They ranged in age from twelve to four years old. My grandmother, Melba, was just thirty-eight and my grandfather, Merle, was forty-two.

All the children were born in Lewiston, Maine. When they were still very young, my grandmother became seriously ill. The doctors thought she might have tuberculosis, so they sent the children to orphanages for a time while my grandmother recovered. It was the only way my grandfather could keep working. The kids weren't quite sure who went where, but they knew they weren't together for a while.

Eventually they all reunited and moved to Boston. Despite my visions of lace-bordered tablecloths and heirloom teapots, it was the early 1930s and the Great Depression hit them hard like most everyone else. My grandfather had connections in Boston because he was born nearby in Everett, Massachusetts. Connections meant possible work, so they moved. But things must not have panned out as they'd hoped, because in 1934 they would need to move again. The desperation of that time was a strange and powerful motivator, and like so many other people, they would cross a continent in search of something better.

Incredibly, my grandmother went first. By bus. By herself. Her brother Don Oliver was a police officer in Los Angeles, and he would help her find work and get settled. She did both. Then, some time later, my grandfather left their car in Boston and loaded his six children on a bus bound for the west coast. He was a machinist in the Navy and both North American Aviation and Northrop in Inglewood were hiring in the early run-up to World War II.

They apparently did well in their new life and in 1936, they moved to the little house at 571 East Hazel Street in Inglewood. It was a lovely neighborhood, close to schools and just across the street from beautiful Centinela Park.

My grandfather never mentioned the troubled times when talking about their move from Boston. He would tell a *Los Angeles Times* reporter: "We moved here in order that we could raise our children in the fresh air and sunshine of California. We wanted to get them away from the terrific heat of the eastern summers and the intense cold of the winters."

He explained that they had moved to Hazel Street "so that our children could take advantage of their play hours in the nearby park. I felt that this was the best thing we had done for the children since we moved to California."

IT'S STRANGE WHEN I think about it now, but I was born in Inglewood, at Centinela Hospital, near the park. My family had moved to nearby Gardena a few years earlier, but my mom's doctor was still at the Inglewood hospital, so she stayed with him and had me at Centinela. But Gardena is where all my memories begin, including one that makes so much more sense now.

I was about ten years old when a friend and I rode our bikes down to the corner market. We parked our bikes outside and were only in the market for a few minutes. When we came out, as if on cue, a man got out of the passenger's side of a car and approached us. My dad always warned me about strange men, so I noticed him and his timing. But we were on our bikes by now, just getting ready to speed off with our candy. We were going to be fine.

No.

The man came from behind and caught one of my handlebars, said my bike was nice. And it was—a brand-new ten-speed Santa delivered at Christmas.

"How about you let me take it for a little ride?"

"I really shouldn't. We need to go."

He moved in closer and flashed a knife blade near my face while the driver got out of the car and opened the trunk. I felt like I was going to faint or throw up, or both. I don't remember my friend saying or doing anything. We were frozen.

He nudged me with the knife.

I slowly got off the bike and gave it to him. He handed it off to the driver, who quickly put it in the trunk. My friend handed over hers. And then we ran like our lives depended on it. They probably did.

When the police came to our house later, they asked me to describe everything—the men, the car, anything that came to mind. And somehow, I remembered the license plate from that car. The police ran it and later tracked the men down at a nearby warehouse, where they were stockpiling all kinds of stolen property.

I didn't sleep well for months after that. I always thought I was hearing someone walking outside my bedroom window. My stomach hurt all the time. I was afraid to ride my bike or to walk anywhere. Then I was subpoenaed to testify in the thieves' case and I got worse.

But I testified and I can still remember now, decades later, how the prosecutor asked me to identify the men and I did. And then he asked me about the license plate number and I calmly recited "GGW969." I will probably never forget that combination of letters and numbers.

After I testified, my dad said he was proud of me and he always said how lucky my friend and I were that day. "They could have put you two in the trunk of that car." I guess I'd known that at the time, but hearing my dad say it made me even more afraid. I had narrowly escaped something awful.

About a year or so later, my dad announced that we were moving to Reno. I was furious. I was eleven years old and couldn't imagine leaving my friends, my school, my neighborhood, and my older sisters who were married and out of the house but close by so we could visit often. My mom felt the same way. *What about all our friends? What about everything we've built here?*

But he wouldn't hear any of it. He wanted us to have a better life, away from the smog and crime of Los Angeles to the clean air and mountains around Lake Tahoe. I remember him saying, "We're going to a place where you'll be able to ride your bike again."

He must have thought about his dad so many years before, telling him and his siblings about their move from Boston to California, and how he was taking them to a place where they could all play in the mild weather and endless sunshine. Instead, they moved into the clutches of evil. The regret must have consumed my grandparents.

And my dad must have struggled with the fearful hindsight about his father's calamitous decision to move. No wonder my dad wanted to escape Los Angeles and all its memories. Some recent and frightening. Some decades old and absolutely terrifying.

Knowing what I know now, I feel like he moved us to Reno to protect me. He knew what danger lurked in the world, and he wouldn't risk losing his daughter to any of it.

I lost two sisters. I can't lose my daughter.

THE GATHERING STORM

Centinela Park Inglewood, California
Sunday, June 27, 1937

OLIVE AND HER little sisters were at the park on Friday morning, the day before the girls disappeared, when a man who said he was Eddie the Sailor asked Olive to go to a local store and buy a piece of rope so he could do rope tricks for the girls. She'd also seen him throw his wrists out of joint to entertain her and other children at the park. He could fold his hands back flat on his arms and everyone would stare, so amazed. They'd never seen anything like it.

After the rope and wrist tricks that Friday, he asked the girls to go rabbit hunting with him in the Baldwin Hills. He said he had a car. He said he was married and had a daughter. He promised that each girl could bring home her own bunny. Little Marie looked at Olive and begged, *Can we please go, please please can we go?* Olive affectionately punched Marie's arm, gave her a stern look, and then told the man that their mother would never want them to go anywhere with a strange man. He asked again, even telling the girls to meet him early the next morning, but Olive said it was time to leave and the girls hurried home.

They told their mother about Eddie the Sailor and she quickly warned them again about such dangers. She reminded them, as so many parents did, that if they were ever afraid or needed help, they should find a policeman or a fireman, someone who could be trusted. But otherwise, they shouldn't go anywhere with a strange man.

Nine-year-old Marie agreed and piped up: "Gee, Mom, I don't

think Olive should talk to him or go anywhere with him. Just think, she might never come back!"

AT THE EVERETT home on Sunday, while the frenzied search continued, Chief Campbell took his time with Olive. He questioned her slowly, gently. She'd been through so much.

She said Eddie the Sailor had a small black moustache, and on Friday he had been wearing a khaki work shirt and blue bibless overalls. He was younger than Daddy, but she wasn't sure how old. He'd said he lived nearby on Manchester Boulevard, and Olive even remembered the address. She picked out a man from a photo lineup of several mugshots. His name was Othel Leroy Strong.

Three adults, including the park superintendent George Frantz, and several children corroborated her identification. They too said Strong was Eddie the Sailor and they'd seen him in the park on Saturday morning and in the days before the girls had disappeared. One man said he thought Strong was a truck driver and that he drove a 1929 or 1930 Ford roadster with an open box on the back. Edward Knott, an ice deliveryman, had seen an old Ford roadster with no fenders and a rumble seat in front of the park on Saturday morning. He said there were two little girls in the front with a man and one in the box on the rear. He thought the man resembled a photo of Othel Strong.

AS CHIEF CAMPBELL talked with Olive, my grandmother sat nearby, overcome with grief, under a doctor's care, her mind and heart racing. She went over and over it. She just could not believe the girls would go off in a car with a man they didn't know. She had just talked to them about it the day before. "For that reason, I know Marie would come home to me if it were possible," she told Campbell and reporters.

She also remembered how a man tried to lure the two younger sisters and a friend away from the park months earlier in December, but Marie was able to pull the younger girls away from him and they ran home. The Everetts called police but officers told them to not tell anyone about the incident in hopes that the man would try it again and the police could catch him.

She tried to concentrate on the radio, listening for news—any news—that would explain where her little girls had gone. But she kept coming back to the fact that Eddie the Sailor made no sense. They could not have gone with that strange man. Not after what had happened in December and especially not after what had happened on Friday. No, it could not have happened that way. It could not have happened at all.

She politely fended off reporters' continued questions about whether the girls would have gone with Eddie the Sailor. She held a hand to her mouth, choking back tears, and told them, "I'm afraid to let myself think what might have happened to them."

REPORTERS WERE DOWN at the Stephenses' home too. Mrs. Stephens pleaded for the girls' return in a prepared statement:

> *Whoever may have our little girl, please see that she isn't cold or hungry, as she is just dressed in summer dress and underclothing and perhaps hasn't eaten since Saturday at breakfast. Please let the girls free somewhere close enough so that they can get home; don't hurt them as they are really just little girls. Jeanette, if you are free, or if Marie or Madeline can get free, please go to a telephone or ask someone to phone Mrs. Church at Inglewood 1042 and tell her just where you are and how you are. She will come down and tell us about you, then daddy and mother will come after all of you.*

MEANWHILE, POLICE QUICKLY learned that just six months earlier, Othel Leroy Strong had been convicted of contributing to the delinquency of a minor after he accosted a fourteen-year-old girl on an Inglewood street. The district attorney's office originally charged Strong with rape, but he ultimately pled guilty to the lesser charge and was sentenced to probation. He had no other criminal record aside from being arrested twice in Inglewood for public drunkenness.

But with an apparent child predator at large, law enforcement was already under immense pressure to find a suspect, so James Davis, chief of the LAPD, seized the political moment to paint Strong as a typical sex offender who'd received a light sentence and, apparently, the freedom to attack again. He recounted several similar, unsolved child murders, suggesting that Strong, or whoever was in the park that morning, was surely to blame for these horrors.

Virginia Brooks, ravished and murdered in San Diego in March 1931. When they found her body, she was clutching dark black hairs in one hand. She was last seen talking to a man in a 1929 Ford coupe.

Louise Teuber, found nude and hanging from a tree between LA and San Diego in April 1931. She'd been strangled and hung up with a rope that featured complicated nautical knots. Her clothes were arranged in a neat pile nearby.

Nine-year-old Delbert Aposhian, whose mutilated body was found in the San Diego Bay, last seen talking with a dark man at the docks.

And sixteen-year-old Celia Cota, her ravished and strangled body found a half block from her home in 1934. She had white rabbit hairs on her hands.

"This is a good time for public sentiment to strengthen against degenerates," the chief urged at a press conference that day. "Stronger sentences must be imposed upon this type of person. They should be put away so that little children unable to protect themselves can safely play without fear of attack. We have had too many sex crimes in this state in recent years."

The hunt for Othel Strong was on.

THE INGLEWOOD TOWN barber, Claude Coop, was finishing the last of his Sunday morning coffee when he saw his neighbor Albert Dyer coming up the walk bright and early at 6:30. Dyer had stopped by the evening before and told Coop he needed money. The barber said he'd pay Dyer $2 if he helped hoe some weeds, and the pair worked in Coop's yard for several hours. Coop didn't think anything of it because Dyer was always asking for money and favors. He was such an odd bird. Thirty-two years old and always out of work. He'd been working as a crossing guard for the WPA for the last six months or so, but he still never had any money. All the men in the barbershop thought Dyer was a little crazy because he'd usually sit in the chair and ramble incoherently. They always said it would be terrible if Dyer were locked up in a sanitarium with nothing but his own thoughts. Crazy but harmless, that's how he was.

The next day, Monday, the *Los Angeles Times* hit newsstands early with the chilling front page headline "Three Children Feared Kidnapped; Hundreds of Police Join Hunt: Girls Believed Lured Away By Stranger." Just below the headlines, above the fold, photos of the three girls. Marie and Madeline standing together in one, and Jeanette Stephens standing and holding a stuffed animal in the other. The sunny settings, three happy smiles, and the cheery little dresses, all in stark contrast to the grim caption suggesting the unimaginable.

Dyer showed up at Coop's shop for a haircut. He was in a hurry.

"The WPA's ordered us up to the Baldwin Hills to help hunt for the bodies of those poor kids," Dyer said urgently.

"Bodies? Do they know what happened to those girls?" Coop wondered.

"I don't think so. It's just that they've been gone for a couple days now, up in the hills."

"Well, we better get you taken care of so you can get up there."

Coop shook his head. Three little girls. What was the world coming to?

FIFTH GRADE

Centinela Elementary School, Inglewood, California
1936–1937 School Year

FIFTH GRADE TEACHER Mrs. Bragg liked to change the students' seats every two weeks to be sure everyone got to know each other. During the latest shuffle, Howard Hilborn ended up sitting next to Marie Everett. He thought to himself how she was so giggly, just like all the other girls.

And then out of the blue: "Marie, will you please come to the front of the class?" Mrs. Bragg asked, but with a knowing tone that made it sound more like an order than a question.

"Yes, Mrs. Bragg," as little Marie walked to the front and turned to face her classmates. She held her hands together respectfully in front of her and looked up at Mrs. Bragg.

The classroom quieted as students wondered what was happening. Poor Marie! Howard felt so bad for her, getting called in front of everyone like that. But then he realized that she wasn't even nervous. She was just fine.

"Class, Marie is going to sing a song for us today, a song her mother taught her. Listen carefully please because we're all going to learn the song together. Marie?"

Marie smiled confidently and never hesitated. "I'm going to sing 'The Spanish Cavalier' by William Hendrickson."

And in a beautiful, clear voice, she began, instantly losing herself in the music.

Howard and the rest of the class were thinking about what it took to get up and sing like that in front of everyone. They all thought the same thing—Marie Everett was brave. So very brave.

ALONE

The Baldwin Hills above Inglewood, California
Monday, June 28, 1937

SEVERAL MILES ABOVE the city, the girls' bodies lay in a deep, narrow gulley at the base of a ravine. Three pairs of little shoes lay there, too, placed in a neat row on the sand, two pairs facing one way, the third pair facing the other way. Someone had taken greater care with the shoes than with the bodies.

Jeanette had come to rest facedown with one arm outstretched and the other under her head, as if she was sleeping. The rope was pulled so tightly around her neck, it was just several inches around, efficiently knotted at the back. Her dress was thrown over her head, her bloody legs and torso exposed. She was at a low point at the north end of the canyon.

Seventy-five feet up the canyon, little Madeline was left facedown beneath the thick brush, dried weeds and grasses sprinkled over parts of her. Another rope, just inches around her tiny neck.

And another forty feet farther up the canyon, Marie was also facedown, partially covered with the same weeds and grasses. Her hair was tousled forward and to the side, stuck to her face with dried blood and mud. Her right hand was at her neck, a finger caught in the rope. Her fight to stay alive, her desperate attempt to escape—her unanswered pleas—all frozen in time.

ACCORDING TO MY Aunt Olive, Marie had said something several times in April and May of 1937, months before she and Madeline were killed. "If anything ever happens to me, look up at the moon and the stars and that's where I'll be."

She must have known that people would be searching for her someday, like me, seventy-five years later.

Researching my family's story was difficult, but not just for the obvious reason of having to learn about the tragedy and the pain so many endured. I also struggled sometimes with feeling sort of detached, or something I couldn't quite name. I never knew the girls, never even knew they existed; no names, no photographs, nothing. So, even though I could feel for them, as anyone could, I still wasn't connecting to them as family, and I wondered if I ever would, because, other than their deaths, I had nothing to bring me closer to them.

Then I learned that they'd been buried in unmarked graves. I assumed my grandparents hadn't wanted media and strangers at the grave. Times were tough then, but they could have afforded something, so it must have been the privacy issue, which only added insult to injury—the very thing designed to keep strangers away would also keep family from ever knowing the truth, and from ever being able to get close to the girls in the only way that was still possible. I felt sure no one had visited their graves except my grandparents, and maybe even they avoided going to escape reliving it all.

Thinking of their forgotten lives, something changed for me, something in my relationship to these girls who were my aunts, my dad's little sisters. It was just so tragic, to have died as they did and then to be buried away—literally—as if they never lived at all.

They'd been alone so long.

I wanted to make things right if I could, so I contacted the Inglewood Park Cemetery, explained the situation: they were murdered, buried in 1937, the graves may be unmarked. I was on hold for some time.

"Miss Everett, I'm sorry but they're not here. Jeanette Stephens is here, but the Everett girls are not."

"How did you know to check on Jeanette Stephens?" I hadn't mentioned her.

"When people heard me looking into the records of the Everett girls, they remembered the case, and so we looked for Jeanette too."

"Are you sure they're not there?"

"Yes, Miss Everett, I'm sure. I'm sorry."

It took weeks to get death certificates. I was rushing off to the store one day, picked up the mail, and brought it with me in the car. I thumbed through it when I got to the store parking lot, finding the letter from the records division in Norwalk, California.

Melba Marie Everett, DIED June 26–28, 1937, FOUND June 28, 1937. Cause of death: Strangulation. "By rope tied very tightly about the throat." Homicide. Madeline P. Everett. Homicide.

And I felt something deepen again, but wondered, how was a death certificate—the most sterile and cold account of any death—stirring such emotions? Then, there at the bottom, was the cemetery information: Forest Lawn. And I knew I was finally feeling some sort of connection, because I was trying to find them, not just their vital statistics, but *them*, all these decades later. I called Forest Lawn and a wonderfully helpful clerk found both of their records.

"They're interred together in the old Graceland section, and no, it appears there are no headstones."

I worked tirelessly, feeling uneasy every day that went by knowing where they were and with nothing to mark their memories. I looked into various designs with a Los Angeles monument company and called Forest Lawn for information on how to get the two headstones set. The representative said she'd email me the information. Instead, she called a bit later and asked if I'd gotten her email yet. Had I gotten the photos yet?

What photos?

I opened her email and there they were—two simple bronze markers with the girls' full names—Melba Marie Everett and Madeline Phyllis Everett. No specific dates, just the birth and death year for each: 1928–1937 and 1929–1937. Nothing else. My grandparents took care of them after all. They'd probably bought what they could afford, or maybe they couldn't afford anything and they bought what they simply couldn't live without. But what a sweet sight.

I'd found them. Or maybe they'd found me.

AROUND THIS SAME time in my research process, I was talking by phone with a clerk at the Los Angeles Public Library when she said rather suddenly, and in a somber tone, "We have pictures of your family, about twenty of them." I wasn't surprised that the library had plenty of photos about the case, but I hadn't expected many of my family, always assuming the reporters of the day would have given them a wide berth during those agonizing days and nights when the girls were still missing. I was wrong.

The library sent copies of the photographs by mail a couple of weeks later and as I started opening the package, I felt like I was invading their privacy somehow. I was about to see things beyond the newspaper headlines, images of that time they could never talk about, images they never wanted me to see or know about, scenes from their home where time must have stood still while they waited for news.

Indeed, the first photo was of their house, a little place on East Hazel Street in Inglewood, across from Centinela Park. And sitting on the front stoop were my Aunt Olive and Uncle Carl. The photo was dated June 28, 1937.

I recognized my Aunt Olive's face—the same face I would know well so many years later, when she was forty-something and came to my grandmother's legendary Christmas Eve celebrations, where kids were king and the presents flowed endlessly from some magic spigot under the tree. There she was. Back in time, an eleven-year-old girl, wondering, worrying when—if—her little sisters would ever come home.

I studied my Uncle Carl, who'd been a six-foot-five giant to me, a tough lineman for the telephone company, my dad's burly hunting companion, and my favorite uncle because he was always smiling, as if he'd never experienced a moment of sadness or misfortune in his life. But in the archive photos, he was staring at the camera with a mix of bewilderment and pleading. I suspect he was waiting for news not because he understood what was happening but because he understood that everyone else was waiting for something. Maybe he was thinking the men with the big flashbulbs were there to help. Maybe they could make Mommy stop crying. Carl was only five years old.

And then the cameramen had moved inside the house and the second photograph was the first real picture of my grandfather I'd seen.

I never met him. He died long before I was born. The only things I knew about him I learned through my dad. My grandfather's core values—honesty, integrity, education, hard work, and all those other "Bostonian" principles—lived on in my dad. When he scolded me about some departure from those values, he'd quote my grandfather, and I felt like there was an invisible elder passing judgment on me. I feared the ghost of Merle Everett and his impossible standards.

I found more evidence of those standards in some family mementos, like his Navy discharge certificate from 1921, with an "Enrollment Record" and ratings for his service. Two of the categories were "sobriety" and "obedience." He scored a perfect 4.0 on both. Of course. He hardly seemed human.

And the few photos I'd seen of him over the years did nothing to change that perception. They were taken late in his life and he always looked very much the old grandfather, perpetually serious and, in hindsight, heavily burdened. He was clearly the stern taskmaster who'd apparently made my dad so strict with me.

But this man in the photograph from 1937 was someone completely different.

I was taken aback by how young he was—only forty-two—and by the emotion in his eyes. I'd been researching and reading about someone I'd never known, someone I always pictured as old and staid, but there he was, this gentle, brokenhearted young father.

He's holding little Carl on his lap, looking into his eyes, a knowing arm around his body, uncomfortably aware of the prying lenses but maintaining Carl's gaze to communicate calm and comfort—*you are safe with me, we will be okay*. His shirt collar is open, he has the slightest five o'clock shadow, and he looks like a man who is trying to hide his desperation from his remaining children but who will surely begin weeping as soon as he's alone. He told reporters later that day how the suspense was killing him and his family but that he'd gone to the garage to break down so my grandmother wouldn't see him.

The rest of the photographs were equally moving—scenes from the girls' bedroom with their toys and blanket from the park, a corner table in my grandparents' house with the girls' picture and a large spray of flowers and my grandmother's hat pin and clutch laid just so, near the flowers, a shrine for the missing. And despite years of research that left no doubt about my family's tragedy, these photographs—much like the girls' death certificates—deepened my connection to the story. I could see in these images people I'd really known, touched, heard and loved, and I began looking at the photographs, and the story, more as a granddaughter, a daughter and a niece. I saw more clearly how it had really happened—to all of them.

But again, there were no photographs of my dad, no sign that he was even there during those days, those hours, before all hope left our family.

THE BOY SCOUTS

The Baldwin Hills above Inglewood, California
Monday, June 28, 1937

SIXTEEN-YEAR-OLD FRANK PORTUNE and his group of eight Boy Scouts from Inglewood Troop 203 had been searching for the girls since Saturday night. On Monday, they were assigned to go deeper into the Baldwin Hills, to areas beyond the access roads. About 9:00 a.m., they established a contact point near Slauson and LaBrea and then moved off in detachments through the bean fields and rugged oil-drilling areas. Portune was with fifteen-year-old Patrol Leader Horace Card, thirteen-year-old Bob Brown, and his fourteen-year-old brother, Albert Portune.

Holding fast to scout rules, the trio marched through the hills, stopping to check out suspicious ravines and washes, and checking under shrubs and bushes. They worked all day and even though they tired, they were determined to keep searching as long as the girls might need their help.

Around 2:00 p.m., after scouting nearly six miles, they came to a ridge with a steep, deep ravine about fifty feet below. It was covered almost entirely with heavy brush, and the boys thought it might be a good hiding place.

The scouts half-slid, half-stumbled down the steep bank, clutching at chaparral and wild oats to stay on their feet. As they reached the gully floor, Portune came around a bend in the gully wall and froze.

He saw Marie's feet and then her blood-specked legs and the rope tight around her neck, only a couple of inches around.

The other scouts looked on in horror, their stomachs reeling and unpredictable. They knew the other girls' bodies might be close by, but the ravine was so choked with shrubbery and undergrowth that a search might take too long—too long when they knew they had to get word back to the police.

Another patrol of five scouts was close behind and quickly arrived at the scene, agreeing to stand watch while Portune's group went for help. The boys ran as fast as they could, walking only when they needed to catch their breath. They finally came to a highway and flagged down an oil worker with a car who drove them to the contact point, where they caught a ride into town to the Inglewood police station. Portune and his friends were breathless and wild-eyed as they reported their find.

IT WAS EERILY quiet as the teams of investigators surveyed the scene. The silence was punctuated only by mumbled expressions of disbelief, the click and whine of the police cameras and the sounds of brush beneath the men's boots. The men, many of them seasoned professionals with years of experience at crime scenes, had never seen anything like it. Most were rendered speechless when they saw those girls. Strangled and mercilessly violated from what appeared to be multiple, repeated sexual assaults. Adding to the horror was the fact that none of the investigators could tell if the assaults had been pre- or post-mortem. They must have silently prayed for the latter.

When they lifted Marie's body, they found a little bag under her tortured corpse. It was the type of bag drugstores used for prescription medicines. An officer carefully collected it.

As the men started to move the bodies from the ravine, most removed their shoes to keep from sliding on the wild oats and dry grass. One of the men wondered aloud if the killer maybe told the girls to take off their shoes for the same reason. He could have explained that he didn't want them to slide too far down the ravine but done so knowing they couldn't escape as easily with their shoes off. The other men shook their heads in continued horror.

Just up from where they found Marie's body, closer to the

entrance to the ravine, an investigator found the thermos of milk and Madeline's Mickey Mouse book.

About a half mile away, another investigator stumbled on a pair of denim overalls. They appeared to have blood on them.

I WONDERED ABOUT the moment when my grandparents first heard the news—who told them, and how? Did they shield my grandmother or did she and my grandfather learn the truth together, in a spare office at the police station, or at home, with reporters no doubt lurking outside hoping to get the first glimpse of reaction? For some reason, I always pictured a police officer and perhaps a doctor walking somberly toward their front door, prepared to deliver news of the unimaginable. But the reality, at least according to the press, was far different.

Someone first delivered the news to Jeanette's mother down the street. A neighbor then ran impulsively to the Everett house and told my grandfather what he'd heard down at the Stephenses' place. In disbelief, my grandfather fled to the Inglewood police station to find out about the search, but officers there confirmed the worst and he would have to return home to tell my grandmother.

Reporters documented the cruel chain of events:

> *"I could not believe the officers at first,"* Everett, trembling and near collapse, said after he had returned to his wife.
>
> *"Finally one convinced me that it was true and then—"* here his body was wracked by sobs.
>
> *"—A stranger walked into the station. He did not know me. He told in detail of the discovery of the little bodies. He spared no detail.*
>
> *"He told of the position in which my children, my little girls, lay. He spoke of their little shoes and socks being found nearby. His descriptions nearly drove me mad.*
>
> *"I could stand no more. I rushed from the station. I had to tell my wife. But I could hardly tell her. I was stunned. I could hardly believe it myself."*

And when the mother learned from her husband's lips that the children were dead, she again broke into sobs and was overcome by hysteria.

Beside her, the father—a man who had waited through the long hours of two nights for word of his girls—fell silent in strange contrast to the pitiful grief of his stricken wife.

Shocked into silence, he was unaware of the crowds that gathered in front of his home.

THE MOB

Inglewood City Hall, California
Monday, June 28, 1937

ON MONDAY NIGHT, as the search for the girls transitioned to a manhunt for the killer, a mob amassed in front of the police station at Inglewood City Hall, threatening to lynch the monster who committed what Los Angeles District Attorney Buron Fitts was calling the "most fiendish crime in the whole annals of Los Angeles County."

The army was more than 1,500 strong—men and boys from all walks of Inglewood life. Fathers and brothers, friends and co-workers all came in groups, like the men who worked in the nearby Van Hoven bean fields, who called themselves the Bean Field Gang. Theresa Zeigler's brother Al was one of them, and he joined a group who vowed to go to City Hall every night until the killer was found. Theresa had played with the girls in the park that Saturday morning, and Al knew firsthand what the shock of the murders was doing to families all over Inglewood. The Ziegler parents were so nervous all the time. They were always reverting to speaking their native Italian so the kids couldn't understand what they were saying. There were people out everywhere talking about those little girls.

The mob surged and roared, and rumors swirled that they were digging a pit in which to burn the lynched body. News leaked that they planned to hang the killer from the girls' pepper tree. It was still very warm out after another hot June day and the mob seethed. Some of the men passed around bottles of liquor, like fuel on a fire.

The apparent ringleader demanded justice and rallied action as police brought suspects into the station for questioning.

"That's the bird, let's lynch him! The dog deserves to die!" he cried.

The DA's Investigator Eugene Williams, who was part of the interrogating team, tried to control the crowd. He stepped out in front of Inglewood City Hall and began shouting: "We believe we know who did this!"

The crowd went wild.

"Then give him to us!" one man shouted back.

Williams tried to keep a lid on things. "It isn't going to do any good to congregate here. We'll take care of this fellow when we catch up with him. You can back us up when he's being tried. Now go home."

But the mob carried on. They wanted justice for those little girls.

CHIEF CAMPBELL HAD his hands full when fourteen-year-old Mike Huerta arrived at police headquarters needing to talk. The chief had twelve known degenerates in custody already and more leads were coming in every hour.

Huerta told Campbell that one of the street crossing guards near Centinela Park tried to get him to go for a walk and he'd tried to get other boys to go, too.

Huerta also explained that the man was usually on Inglewood's main street in the evenings, especially Saturday nights. But he wasn't there the previous Saturday night at his usual time and when he finally showed up that night, he seemed strange, jumpy, looking over his shoulder all the time. He kept checking the newspapers.

The chief thought about it and realized he was familiar with the man Huerta had described. During the search, after they'd found the girls, a WPA crossing guard had used his WPA badge to get as close as possible to the bodies. It was probably nothing, but Campbell couldn't leave any stone unturned.

THE CRIMINAL PROFILE

Inglewood, California
Evening, Monday, June 28, 1937

AS EVENING FELL, major newspapers prepared to go to press for the next day's morning editions. The *Los Angeles Times* reporters penned details of "what is expected to be the most intensive man hunt in the history of California." The front-page headlines of the *Los Angeles Examiner* would blare the next day of a "Great Manhunt Launched for Slayer of Three Girls," and "Mob Violence Threatens," dubbing the search "California's greatest manhunt since the Hickman case" a decade earlier, when little Marion Parker, the young daughter of a prominent Los Angeles banker, was abducted from school. The *San Francisco News* would also headline the case and the swelling crowds in Inglewood— "Mob Fury Spreads in L.A. Suburb"—informing its readers of police blockades throughout southern California, with officers watching key bridges and highways in the northern part of the state. And the next day's papers would also deliver the news everyone must have been fearing about the timing of the sexual assaults. The descriptions were sparing but nonetheless horrifying: "Outraged, Then Killed." "Ravished and Garrotted." "Trio Attacked, Strangled."

As the case unfolded on the ground and in the press, and with the Inglewood mob raging on, investigators knew they needed to tap every resource. So, they welcomed Dr. Joseph Paul de River, a psychiatrist who consulted with the LAPD and who had an almost suspicious interest—certainly unique for the time—in sex crimes. After reviewing the girls' bodies at the medical examiner's lab and the physical evidence from the scene, de River provided police with a psychiatric sketch of the killer—a report that would become one of the earliest recorded forensic sex offender profiles in the United States. Dr. de River wrote:

> *Look for one man, probably in his twenties, a pedophile who might have been arrested before for annoying children. He is a sadist with a superabundance of curiosity. He is very meticulous and probably now remorseful, as most sadists are very apt to be masochistic after expressing sadism. The slayer may have a religious streak and even become prayerful. Moreover, he is a spectacular type and has done this thing, not on sudden impulse, but as a deliberately planned affair. I am of the opinion that he had obtained the confidence of these little girls. I believe they knew the man and trusted him.*

ARRANGEMENTS

571 East Hazel Street, Inglewood, California
Tuesday, June 29, 1937

THE DRESSES FLOAT like ghosts, suspended on wire hangers in the doorframe of my grandparents' living room. Newspaper photographers captured the shot and learned from someone that my grandmother was trying to decide which of the dresses to send to the funeral home. My family had begun the painful, reluctant shift from waiting for their girls to making funeral arrangements for them. It would be the first step in trying to move on to whatever life comes after losing two young children.

My dad used to tell me to be kind to others "because you never know what people are going through, what burdens they might be carrying." Like so many other things he used to say, I think about this one differently now. He knew the secret burden his family carried and he felt its weight. But I think he was especially worried about what my grandmother had endured and how it must have darkened her days. He spent so much time with her when I was growing up, taking her grocery shopping, going to her house for tea and a visit, and just including her in our lives.

The side effect for me was getting to spend a lot of time with her. I knew her well and remember so many hours practicing at the piano, sorting jars of jewel-like buttons in her magical sewing room, or both of us in aprons making miniature mincemeat pies—"mincies," we called them—with every conceivable pot, pan, sifter, and utensil out and happily in use. But best of all were so many talks at the kitchen table. My dad loved the kitchen table for conversation, and he got that from my grandmother, because she always gravitated there to chat over tea while she tatted or crocheted her latest handiwork. This was especially true when she'd come to visit when we lived together in Reno, after my parents divorced. She was terrified of flying but she would take the long Greyhound bus ride from Inglewood to be with us. Those kitchen table memories are especially precious to me.

All the sweeter now seeing how she never let on about the tragedy in her past. She didn't avoid difficult topics altogether, either. One day at the kitchen table I asked her how my grandfather died, why I never knew him, why he'd been gone so long. She seemed to steel herself a little before responding, but she clasped her hands just so and explained how he suffered two strokes several years apart, the second of which caused him to go blind in his right eye. One morning after breakfast, he was sitting in his easy chair and he complained of pain over the blind eye and she told him to lie down on the couch while she got him a pillow. "I wasn't even gone a minute," but when she returned, he was unconscious. He struggled to survive in the hospital for twenty-four hours and "then he was just gone." Doing the math many years later, I learned that he lived only twelve years after the girls were murdered. He was fifty-five years old.

I was about thirteen when she told me the story, so I was not altogether sure how to react, but she immediately gave me cues that it was okay to ask and that she was happy to help me with some history. And as always, she put a silver lining on it that came from heaven. "He was a wonderful husband. He had a good life. And he's with God."

But she never mentioned Marie or Madeline, or any of it. The only possible sign of her heartbreak and grief is yet another thing I see differently now. Her arms were always bruised and scratched, bits of dried blood here and there, irritated red areas. She almost always sat with her arms folded, but every so often a hand would go to her arms and she'd scratch and work at her skin. They were forever in a process of injury, healing, and then reinjury. I suppose her nerves never really calmed after 1937, and maybe her grief was trying to find a way out, any way out, since she never let it escape by traditional means—or at least not in anyone's presence.

So, when I looked at the press photographs of her from decades ago, it was different than looking at my grandfather, whom I was meeting for the first time really. I was seeing someone I knew so well, but who looked almost like a stranger because she was at the center of events I still couldn't believe happened. It was like discovering a cheating spouse or someone living a double life, a life they never disclosed.

I believe she could have talked about it—she had the inner strength—but she was always walking a mile in someone else's shoes and worrying about how things might affect them. She wouldn't want to burden anyone else with such a heartbreaking memory, especially not a granddaughter who might fear for her own life after hearing even the most basic outlines of the story. No, it was better to just keep that to herself. God would provide.

COMMUNITY

Inglewood, California
Tuesday, June 29, 1937

PARENTS GATHERED ALL over Inglewood, and California for that matter, and tried to imagine what the Everett and Stephens families were
going through. The crime was just so heinous, so unthinkable in that
simple time. Wives and mothers stood on porches and in kitchens
with arms crossed, nervously rubbing their dress sleeves and holding
hands to mouths, wondering aloud how anyone could bear it. And
especially Mrs. Everett, she lost two children, two little girls. "Doubly
bereaved," as one newspaper headline put it.

As is the case in so many tragedies, everyone wanted to know
what the families were feeling and doing in those dark hours because
everyone wondered what they would do in that situation, how they
would cope if something like that, God forbid, ever happened to
them. The press wanted to get inside those feelings too.

One of the storylines in the *Los Angeles Times* that day read
"Victims' Father Not Vindictive—Everett Wants Slayer Apprehended
Only to Prevent More Crimes."

"We never dreamed that this move meant the deaths of our little
children," my grandfather told reporters the day after the girls' bodies
were found, explaining how the family had moved to California from
Boston less than a year before.

"I am not vindictive because of the tragedy. I am at least glad to
know where our children are in this hour of grief."

What about the manhunt, Mr. Everett?

"I only want to see this fiend captured so that this awful crime cannot be repeated."

He expressed serious concern for his wife and Mrs. Stephens, both of whom were still under a doctor's care.

But another newspaper quoted him as saying, on the very same day, that lynching would be too good for the killer. "I would string him up and tear him to pieces. I told the police that if they let me come near him I will kill him."

It's still hard for me to believe my conservative New England grandfather would have lost his composure like that, but there must have been some truth to the report. The range of emotions was surely a sign of the internal battle, between the need to be stable and controlled for his wife and remaining children, and the need any father would have had to avenge the violence done to his little girls. The pain—its profound depth and intensity, in his marrow almost—must have stabbed him, again and again.

PERHAPS ANTICIPATING MORE uncertainty and deepening grief, the American Legion announced it would conduct a memorial service on Friday, July 2, at the Veterans Memorial Hall in Centinela Park. Commander Al Greenleaf explained that the grieving families wanted complete privacy at the upcoming funerals for their children, so the Legion was providing an outlet for Inglewood citizens to offer their condolences and come together in support of the families.

As the Legion readied for the memorial service, donations poured into the *Inglewood Daily News* offices after interim mayor Everett Simmons issued a proclamation earlier in the day. "As acting mayor of this city, I call upon one and all to contribute, as a sympathetic gesture on the part of the citizens of Inglewood. This is not only to cover part of the burial expenses, but also to help the parents to feel our sympathy in these sad hours."

Within thirty minutes, business owners and neighbors started arriving at the newspaper's offices to help the stricken families. Girl Scouts also went door-to-door with cigar boxes asking for donations,

and despite the desperate times in a worsening depression, people gave, including the neighbors closest to the Hazel Street families who donated a total of $18 the first day. The *Inglewood Daily News* printed each of their contributions. Fred Peckler, 25¢; A.G. French, 75¢; Mrs. B. E. Shaffer, 50¢; Lloyd Brandset, 30¢.

The *Inglewood Daily News* editorial that evening captured the city's multi-layered emotions, describing it as being "stricken with grief at one of the most horrible crimes that ever visited itself on a community," but noting how "the great heart of Inglewood swells and throbs even in the midst of its sorrow."

In addition to feelings of grief, sorrow, and generosity, Inglewood's citizens were afraid for their children. The *Inglewood Daily News* captured that facet of the city's collective mood as well:

> *It will not tolerate delay in meeting the situation with adequate ordinances to handle any like criminal in the future before commission of the crime; it will not tolerate a lack of adequate police protection in the city park. It is in no mood to quibble about the excuses or alibis why these measures have not been done before. Parents of Inglewood children will either require that this protection be afforded or will take matters into their own hands.*

Los Angeles County Sheriff Biscailuz's opinion piece in the *Inglewood Daily News* only fanned the fires of worry and concern. He wrote passionately:

> *It is high time that something be done to put permanently out of circulation these degenerates who are at large, a potential menace to children and girls. Every time a case of this kind occurs, there is agitation for more strict laws to curb these fiends but in a short time it all dies down and nothing is done. If the tragic death of these three little ones should so arouse public sentiment that something really is done they shall not have died in vain.*

A concerned mother, Mrs. B. E. Jarrett, couldn't be troubled with laws. She just wanted police officers on the beat. She pleaded with

Inglewood city council members and made it clear she was doing so as a mother, not as part of any organization.

"If we go to park employees, they say they have no authority to make arrests. By the time our children come home and tell us about these men who molest them, it's too late and often they're too frightened to do more than run home." She demanded that the city put officers in the park. She did not mince words. "It's been a very bad situation there for months." Mrs. Jarrett said her children have frequently come home and told her of certain "hangers on" who seemed to spend most of the time in the park.

"Why can't these men be picked up and kept from molesting our children? From now on do you think, Mr. Mayor, that our children may be able to go to the police in the park with a complaint and get some satisfaction?"

Other parents spoke up, as did representatives of the local Parent-Teachers Association.

Anticipating more fear and anger as the case developed, the Inglewood Council wasted no time. They passed an emergency ordinance that put three more police officers in Centinela Park, effective immediately.

Inglewood parents breathed a collective sigh of at least some relief as the police continued to frantically hunt for the killer.

WHEN I FIRST read that Eddie the Sailor had approached Olive, Marie, and Madeline just the day before the kidnappings, inviting them to go rabbit hunting, I wondered how my grandparents could have possibly allowed the youngest girls to go to the park unattended the very next day. But I assumed that the prior day's incident must have been such a rare occurrence in an otherwise consistently safe place, and they probably didn't want to alarm the girls too much or make their favorite play area off limits. Instead, they gave them the warning about strange men and all the rest. I reminded myself of the era, decades before instant media reports of abductions, Amber Alerts, statistics on the offending patterns of child predators, and how nobody could have expected this horrible crime in such a seemingly benign setting.

Then I learned how the girls had fended off a suspicious man just months earlier in December, and that it was serious enough for my grandparents to report it to police. The police failed to act, deciding instead to lie in wait so they could catch the perpetrator, which should have told my grandparents that police expected the man to return and to try again. I couldn't understand it but, again, I thought maybe after a reasonable period of time, they'd loosened the reins and let the girls return to the park with all the other children.

And soon I read these reports of angry parents who'd been worried about the park situation for some time, who'd reported molestations and "hangers on," and I found it almost inconceivable that my grandparents, or Jeanette Stephens's parents—any parents—would let their children go there alone. But I also read the affidavits of two young girls who were in the park the Friday before my aunts were kidnapped, and how they told one of their mothers that a strange man intercepted them that day on their way to the swimming pool, asking if they wanted to change into their bathing suits in his car. The girls then testified that they were in the park the next day without their parents, so clearly, there was some significant disconnect between the realities in the park and so many parents allowing their children to play there.

I found no reports that criticized or laid blame with the Everett or Stephens parents, perhaps because nobody dared attack them in their grief, or perhaps because, in hindsight, so many other parents had made the same questionable judgments. But I wondered, and still wonder, if my grandparents felt responsible, if they ever went back over it in their minds and saw those events differently, wishing they'd denied the girls some pleasures in exchange for safety, wishing they'd held the reins tight and indefinitely, the way my dad did with me and my sisters. Maybe that's why he was so terribly strict. Maybe he saw his parents assume the best about people and he would spend his life assuming the worst, never for a minute risking his children to dangers, hidden or otherwise.

MANHUNT

State of California
Tuesday, June 29, 1937

THE PRESSURE ON law enforcement—indeed everyone—to find the girls' killer was intense, and incredibly public. California Governor Frank Merriam issued a statement that was published far and wide:

> *A terrible crime has been committed in California. Three inno-cent children have been strangled. The broken bodies of Madeline Everett, Melba Everett and Jeanette Stephens were found in an Inglewood ravine.*
>
> *A fiend is loose.*
>
> *If we are to protect our homes and especially our children, it is the duty of each of us to see that this maniac strangler is appre-hended that he may be brought to proper and legal justice. Rewards may be posted for the capture of this man but the greatest reward coming to anyone for his capture will be in protecting society from further outrages such as this.*
>
> *Law and order can exist only in so far as they bulwark the individual homes and it is the duty of everyone who lives under law and order to see that the perpetrator of this crime is punished to the full extent of the law.*
>
> *As Governor of California, head of its civil officers, I now call upon its peace officers to exert their best efforts to the solution of this crime, the apprehension of this killer.*

Society, in its path of progress, may find, at some later time, a way to deal with such fiends as this before they strike. Our society, under which we this day live, demands that he be captured and dealt with in a severe and orderly manner provided by law.

THE PRESSURES ONLY intensified when police finally found Othel Strong working in a small lumber camp seven miles from Olympia, Washington. He'd worked there several weeks straight, including the entire previous week. Police confirmed his story with multiple people and reviewed various records—time cards and paychecks—showing that Strong was telling the truth.

The man believed to be Eddie the Sailor was 1,500 miles away from Centinela Park when the girls disappeared.

The fiend was still loose.

BACK IN INGLEWOOD, police officer Elmer Cake picked up Mike Huerta that morning about 10:00 and drove him to a crossing where several WPA guards were on duty. He told the boy that as they drove by the crossing guards, Huerta was to say nothing but the word "yes" if the man Huerta had referred to earlier was in the group. As the unmarked police car slowly approached the crossing, Huerta scanned the faces of three guards who were standing together talking. Officer Cake watched the guards to see if they were reacting. As they passed the trio, Huerta looked over at Cake, and said "yes," as instructed. Cake told reporters that Huerta then identified Albert Dyer as the man.

Cake drove Mike Huerta home, told him to remain available for police questioning, and then sped back to the crossing and pulled up close to the three guards.

As Cake got out of his car and approached the men, Dyer cried, "I never killed those children, I never killed them!" Then Dyer took out of his trousers pocket a newspaper clipping with a picture of him in the search party, near the bodies in the ravine. "I even tried to help take their bodies out but they wouldn't let me."

Cake guided Dyer to the waiting car and took the newest suspect in for questioning.

But the interrogation lasted only a half hour. Dyer said he'd been working in his garden all Saturday afternoon after he'd gotten off work, his wife and neighbors would attest. Police chalked him up as one of those harmless nuts who was overly interested in the crime and besides, he didn't even have a car.

Dyer was released.

DESPITE SO MANY early dead ends, police remained hopeful. They had forensic evidence and they planned to use it.

The front page of the *San Francisco News* blared the headline "FINGERPRINTS CLUE TO KILLER." My grandmother's brother and the girls' uncle, Don Oliver, was a fingerprint expert with the LAPD. Immediately after the bodies were found, Oliver reported "definite and clear fingerprints" on the bodies of all three victims.

"It is only a matter of checking these fingerprints with police records. Only a man with a previous record of sex crimes could have done this terrible thing." In a foreshadowing of the future of sex crimes investigations, police zeroed in on anyone with a "morals offense" record, hoping to match fingerprints with those found on the girls' bodies.

And in addition to the multiple state law enforcement agencies working the case, the FBI was at the ready to help. They had no jurisdiction in the case because no federal laws were violated, but FBI local agent J. H. Hanson told reporters the bureau was there in word and deed, needing "only the smallest legal loophole in the case to turn the full force of the Federal authority into action." But in the meantime, "all facilities of the technical departments in Washington—fingerprint files, laboratories, scientists, experts of all types—are available to authorities working on the case."

Investigators reviewed a parade of suspects.

They brought in twenty-two-year-old Joe Strunk of Lawndale, California. He'd been convicted a few months earlier of a morals offense against a fourteen-year-old girl in nearby Gardena. He claimed he'd been on a fishing trip in the high Sierra on June 26.

John Vasquez had a 1929 Ford with no fenders and no running boards and he admitted to driving in the Baldwin Hills that Saturday, but he denied any involvement with the girls.

Twenty-four-year-old Homer West of Bell Gardens put up a fight when investigators tried to question him about the case, and he said he wouldn't be taken without a warrant. His brother agreed and officers were forced to draw guns on the two men to control the situation. Police held West in the Inglewood jail for further questioning.

H. E. Brinkley of Hollywood was indignant as officers hauled him in for questioning. He had an alibi and offered references and claimed he'd never even seen the inside of a jail. But officers were suspicious that he'd recently grown a beard, so they brought him in.

Daniel Pluma of Los Angeles was covered in tattoos and because witnesses at the park said the man they saw had a tattoo or possibly several, police crosshairs fixed on Pluma.

And then there was the man who left a pair of burr-covered trousers at a dry cleaner's shop in Los Angeles. The pants appeared to have blood on them and the shop owner called police. Police sent the pants for chemical analysis and when the man showed up to claim his cleaning ticket, officers took him in.

But nothing panned out. Not one lead.

Not even James Summit, a thirty-seven-year-old ex-sailor who admitted people sometimes called him "Eddie the Sailor." Police hauled him in with great hope that they were on to something, but Summit provided a solid alibi and was quickly released.

But police had two suspects who were at least warranting further investigation. The first was thirty-year-old Charles A. Keefe, whom Van Nuys police found drunk in his old-style Model T Ford without fenders and with a box on the back. Also inside the car, police found a pair of khaki pants and a bundle of insulated wires resembling telephone cord. Keefe told police he'd lived in Inglewood near Centinela Park for three years and he'd been in Inglewood the Saturday of the kidnappings. Van Nuys police eventually reported to the Los Angeles investigation team that they'd found a bloodstained shirt in Keefe's room and detectives were dispatched to the scene to see if they could find more evidence.

The other suspect, Luther Dow, was a shifty ex-con who was arrested with a girl's handkerchief and skate key in his pocket, both of which the Everett parents said could have belonged to their girls. He had scratches on his arms, back, side, and stomach, and some burrs and grass on his clothing. Two women from the park identified him as "positively" the man they saw playing with the girls that morning, and a neighbor of the Everett family backed them up. But Haskell Wright and Ken Hylander, Centinela Park employees, said Dow was absolutely not the man in the park. Police eventually arrested Dow on suspicion of the murders, but they needed a lot more evidence to move forward on him.

Meanwhile, as police were coming up empty-handed in their search for the killer, all the traffic in and out of Inglewood police headquarters had whipped the city hall mob into an even greater frenzy. People were climbing onto roofs of the buildings around city hall just to get a good view of the suspects. Chief Campbell issued an emergency order to prohibit roof access and officers stood guard to keep people on the ground.

A local radio announcer tried to help. KTMR personality Sandy Roth and his engineer set up shop on the sidewalk near the mob and interviewed people through the long nights. He praised people who favored a law-abiding process and he tried to quell people's anger that the police didn't have their man yet. The atmosphere couldn't have been more circus-like and yet so fraught with explosive danger.

At the same time, boy scouts were back at work searching every garage in the city looking for the fenderless Ford roadster. And whenever someone saw the scouts roaming Inglewood's streets, they thought about those three little girls and the horror that still hung over their neighborhoods and their lives.

FRED GODSEY

Inglewood, California
Thursday, July 1, 1937

NO ONE COULD escape news of the triple murder in Inglewood. And until a few days earlier when Othel Strong was cleared, Strong had been the primary suspect—Eddie the Sailor.

But Ray Ward, an Edison company employee who lived in nearby Redondo Beach, knew he'd seen a man before who fit the description. He remembered someone who had worked for him in Utah in 1933. His name was Fred Godsey and Ward remembered that Godsey had a sister who lived in Inglewood.

Ward hated to waste anyone's time, but the image of Godsey just kept nagging at him. He finally called the police.

Officers first tracked down Godsey's estranged wife in Salt Lake City. She explained they'd been married for several years and had a young daughter together, but she'd started divorce proceedings and the last she'd heard from him was a postcard dated May 14 from Ely, Nevada. He wrote that he planned to go on to Elko, Nevada, from there.

She described him as thirty-four years old, about five feet nine, with a slight build and dark hair. He was part Cherokee Indian, with a dark complexion. He played the violin and wrote stories. He'd been an engineer once and was extremely skilled at repairing sewing machines.

But Fred was a heavy drinker and used the drug Barbital. When he was in one of his drinking spells, he became "inhumanely cruel." He beat her and on occasion, threatened to kill her at knifepoint.

He served in the Navy for a time but was dishonorably discharged because of "degeneracy." His wife said he was highly oversexed and was picked up by police several times for molesting girls. He served time in Utah's State Prison. In fact, he had just been paroled in January 1937 after serving some time for his latest offense of burglary.

He was good at card tricks. He was also very crafty with his hands and liked to entertain children with his antics.

He occasionally visited his sister in Inglewood.

Oh, she added, people called him "Freddie the Sailor."

THE GODSEY LEAD could have been just another tip in what seemed like an endless line of dead ends, but then police saw his photograph. He was almost a dead ringer for Othel Strong.

The police launched into action. Several witnesses who had identified Strong now agreed that Godsey's photograph looked even more like Eddie the Sailor than any other photographs they'd seen.

The *Los Angeles Times* ran Godsey's photo on Friday, July 2, and the next day John Reynolds and John Veltrie, employees of a feed store, went to the police saying Godsey sold them a goat the morning the girls disappeared. They said he was driving a 1928 or 1929 Ford roadster with a box on the back and no top or fenders. Godsey secured the goat in the back of the Ford with a clothesline-type rope. The *Times* reported that investigators considered the goat-clothesline connection important because the police chemist, Mr. Pinker, had found animal hairs on the ropes used to strangle the children. He was reportedly comparing hairs taken from the goat the men bought from Godsey to hairs found on the ropes.

Margaret Rigby told police that yes, Godsey was the man she'd seen running past her house with blood on his clothes late Saturday afternoon.

Ferdinand North, supervisor at Centinela Park, identified Godsey as the man he'd seen in Centinela Park before and on the day of the murders. So did little Ethylyn "Amy" Lancey, who'd been playing in the park on Saturday. And Al Blythe, who also worked at the park, identified Godsey as the man who turned his wrists back against his arms and entertained children with other tricks. Blythe said Godsey looked exactly like Eddie the Sailor.

And perhaps most telling, Olive Everett agreed he was the man who'd talked to her Friday in the park, the one who could flip his wrists back on his arms. The man who said he had a wife and daughter, and a car.

Dr. Wagner, the autopsy surgeon working on the case, commented that "not one man in 10,000 can dislocate his wrists in that manner."

A team of investigators told reporters that Godsey was the most wanted man in the whole investigation. District Attorney Fitts said, "We will make every effort to have this man taken into custody at once. Every law enforcement agency in the West is being notified to be on the watch for Godsey."

The hunt was on again.

GOOD-BYE

Los Angeles and Glendale, California
Friday, July 2, 1937

A FEW YEARS after my parents and I moved to Reno, they decided to get divorced. When they told me, they tried to package the news with a silver lining. I would be able to move with my mom back to Los Angeles, back to my older sisters and friends. My dad would stay in Reno and sell the house, and then figure out his future from there. It would all be fine. But it sure didn't feel that way. It felt awful. My parents, all three of us, had not been good together for a while, but my mom had been especially toxic, and I'd always felt bad watching how my dad struggled so hard to make things work.

A couple days after their announcement, I found my dad out in his garage woodshop. He glanced over and said, "Hi, honey" before turning back to his work.

I visited him there often and usually answered his typical greeting with a "Hi, Dad, whatcha doin'?" But this time I was so nervous, trying to find the right moment to speak up. My chin quivered and I stared at the floor. He quickly realized something was wrong and turned to me with full attention.

"Pamie? What is it?"

Finally, I was able to choke out the words. "Dad, can I please stay here and live with you?"

I realize now that a lot of fathers might have said no, not wanting to raise a teenage daughter without a mother, or maybe not wanting to be hemmed in post-divorce as a single parent. But my dad never hesitated. He left his workbench, kneeled down and hugged me, and told me we'd find our way together. He thanked me for wanting to stay with "your old dad," and for mustering the courage to ask.

And we did find our way, happily, and all because he was the best father anyone could ask for. He healed wounds left by my mom and made me feel loved and protected. He changed my life by saying yes that day and then by creating a life for us together. I'm so grateful for those years I had with my dad. They were some of the happiest in my life.

And while I wish he could have told me more about his sisters, I see that it was only our circumstances that led him to tell me anything at all. We had ended up in an unexpected lifeboat together, and I suppose he wanted me to understand why he was so strict all those years with me and my sisters, being extra-protective as he and I moved forward in our new life alone together, like when he showed up at my boyfriend's house to take me home. Now I do understand. He told me just enough to protect himself and the long-buried story. But perhaps he also told me enough to one day lead me to the little shoes and our family's history. To one day lead me to Marie and Madeline.

PICTURES OF YOUR family. About twenty of them.

At the mortuary, the little gray caskets are just below the mural of the lambs near the church nave. Flowers are everywhere. Huge sprays and wreaths on easels line the entire wall behind the caskets. Smaller vases and pots are on the floor below and enormous ribboned arrangements cascade over each of the little coffins. My grandmother is hidden from those who have come to mourn with her. She sobs in a small curtained alcove, my grandfather's hand closed over hers.

Later, outside, the stone-faced men wheel the closed caskets on draped platforms from the church to the waiting hearse, pallbearers readying to lift the first one while more pallbearers attend the second one and watch with sad solitude, waiting their turn, wondering how the sun could be shining so brightly on this darkest of days.

The graveside service is on a hill at Forest Lawn in Glendale, and the friends and family stand back, behind a row of empty chairs.

They look on in quiet empathy and helplessness as my grandmother stands sobbing, her hands to her face, just below her black hat, one hand clutching her handkerchief, the other flat against her cheek in disbelief and denial. On her right, her brother Don shades her with an umbrella and holds her arm while my grandfather uses both hands to support her other side. His face is pained, he looks almost bewildered, and he stares emptily at one of the caskets as it lies next to the open flower-lined grave.

Then they are rushing my grandmother down the hill, her brother again on her right and my grandfather on her left, both holding elbows, watching their steps, and hers. A mortuary attendant walks just off to the side, hurrying them to a waiting car. The crowd still at the graves behind them watches with pained expressions as the group flees down the hill. The newspapermen are positioned on the hill below the graves, hoisting their huge cameras and flashbulbs as the family rushes past them.

My grandfather's mouth is partially open. I hear him saying something, trying to comfort his overwrought wife. *Honey, I've got you, just a few more steps. We're almost there, I've got you, I've got you.*

My grandmother is covering her entire face with both hands. I can hear her sobbing. I can see her shoulders heaving. I can hear her muffled cries as she's lifted along, almost stumbling, down the hill, away from her girls. *No, no, no. Please God no.*

ON THIS VERY day when my family's wounds were laid so open, their grief at its painful apex, the American Legion memorial service planned for that evening in Inglewood—the community's attempt at healing—was canceled. The *Inglewood Daily News* reprinted the written statement that was tacked up at Veterans Memorial Hall:

> *The Legion is in full accord with the program to erase the horrible memory of the tragedy from the minds of the citizens of Inglewood, and although it will insist that steps be taken and continued to prevent a recurrence of the tragedy, the organization does not propose to keep the memory of it alive longer than necessary.*

A "program" to erase the horrible memory. We do not propose to keep the memory alive longer than necessary. We will erase it. Like it never happened.

Is that what my family did? Is that what they had to do? The crime against them and the Stephens family reminded people—or taught them for the first time—what horrors might lurk in seemingly innocent settings. The town's beloved park. Near the swimming pool. On a picnic blanket. Three little girls.

So perhaps my grandparents, and even my dad—who refused to wear a red baseball hat once because it would draw too much attention—felt ashamed and embarrassed. Did we invite this? Did we cause all this? Surely these things don't happen to good God-fearing people. It was all so unseemly.

And so we will erase it. We will not keep it alive.

Times have changed and now we often heal collectively, supporting victims whose lives are upended when tragedy strikes down the street or across town. But how did my grandparents feel when they read that passage, when they learned their community was not willing to come together because it might keep their story alive?

Then again, maybe they asked for the event to be canceled. *We appreciate your efforts but you should not have to grieve with us for any longer than is necessary. We will use your kindness for strength, but we release you to return to your lives, to begin the path back to normalcy. We will take it from here. The memories will live on only in us. You may erase them. Thank you. God bless.*

THE CIRCUS

Inglewood, California
July 2–4, 1937

IT'S HARD TO imagine a triple-murder case involving three young girls and triggering one of the largest manhunts in California history unfolding without television, but it did, and the news still spread like wildfire with stories in newspapers and radio broadcasts across the country. And the 1937 reporters proved just as invasive and aggressive as today's cable TV hounds, and inevitably they found people looking for their fifteen minutes of fame.

On July 2, while my grandparents buried their daughters, Hollywood psychic La Reina Rule toured the crime scene—Centinela Park, the route to the bean field, and the ravine. When Rule reached the bean field, she pointed to a spot in the road and said the killer stopped his car there and the trio had gone down that side of the canyon.

"He never returned to Inglewood—he climbed back this way to his car, drove it out on this dirt road." Rule followed the road to Higuera Street, looked west, and said, "This is the way he went—he's at one of the beach cities. I can see a small red farmhouse. It's on an east-west street near the ocean. I think he's spent a lot of time in San Pedro, the house may be there.

"As I see this man, he is staying close to the house. He's with a short, heavy fat man with a pasty face—a man with perverted tendencies. This fat man is more repulsive looking than the murderer and in his forties.

"The murderer has shaved off his moustache—and I think he is wearing women's clothes as a disguise. Sooner or later he will return to the scene of the crime—perhaps wearing the feminine garb. The murderer has trouble with both his legs, feet or ankles and his teeth are not good—some are missing."

The *Los Angeles Times* ran the story on July 3, and the reporter who accompanied Rule said that "at her insistence" he gave her no suggestions about the sites or the case. But that wouldn't have been necessary—the story was front-page news for several days with many references to the park, the ravine, disappearing moustaches, and would-be suspects, including Fred Godsey. Following up on Rule's references to San Pedro and the heavyset man, I found another curious interview.

Burt Sorrenson owned an awning store in Inglewood and he claimed that Godsey came to his shop just before Christmas looking for work repairing sewing machines. Sorrenson described a 1929 Ford roadster with a box on the back and a "fat companion" who always remained in the background, never revealing his identity. Sorrenson told reporters that he, Sorrenson, and Godsey had a falling-out when Godsey showed up at the store "drunk or doped."

Sorrenson went to the *Los Angeles Times* with his news the night of July 3, after the psychic story ran in the same paper that day. Raising even more suspicion about Sorrenson's information was the fact that, at least according to records I reviewed, in December 1936, Fred Godsey was still in the Utah State Prison serving time for burglary. He was not paroled until January 1937.

Still, Rule and Sorrenson added a few twists to the emerging story, and police, desperate for leads because a child-killer was at large, would take anything they could get.

Police recalled a report from H. D. Roberts of the County Welfare Department of a man who matched the killer's description and appeared to have freshly shaved his moustache on Sunday morning and who was traveling with a fat, pasty-faced man.

"The man was highly nervous. He said he was broke and signed a fictitious name and address on the sales slip. He told me he'd been drunk the night before and asked wringing his hands, 'Do you think I can drive all right?'" Roberts said he asked the man why the heavy fellow in the car didn't drive for him, and the man said, "He's sick, he can't."

Then there was George Ray. The twenty-five-year-old man went to police on July 2 with what he said was game-changing information.

Ray told investigator Sanderson how the WPA crossing guard Albert Dyer talked to him Monday night outside the Inglewood police station after the girls' bodies were brought in but before the autopsy was performed. And Dyer knew things about the condition of the bodies that nobody could have known at that point—not even the medical examiners.

Ray explained that he was an employee at the clinic where the autopsies were performed and that he was troubled by the details Dyer seemed to know. Dyer just had too much "positive information," Ray said.

Police dismissed the report for several reasons—Dyer was with the search party at the ravine and he saw the bodies there, and more importantly, police had already questioned Dyer early in the case. Yes, it was strange that Dyer was in the Baldwin Hills trying to be part of the search party, but investigators had seen Dyer as a dim bulb who thought he was a cop because of his WPA badge.

Police and the media learned later that George Ray first tried to sell his information about Dyer to a newspaper that was offering a reward for information leading to the killer's capture, but they refused Ray because Dyer had already been questioned and released. Ray finally gave up and went to police a full five days after the claimed meeting with Dyer.

ALBERT DYER BURST into investigation headquarters without warning early the evening of July 2.

"What do you fellas want with me?" Dyer demanded.

The investigators looked at Dyer, then each other. The silence must have been awkward until Chief Williams told Dyer, "Take a seat over there, we'll be with you in a moment."

Dyer waited while investigators recalled who he was and remembered that they'd questioned him earlier in the case and released him, making his sudden appearance all the more suspicious.

Dyer again demanded, "I want to know what you fellas want with me. I was questioned once in this case and completely cleared. What are you after me again for?"

"But we're not looking for you."

And Dyer left.

LAPD Lieutenant Sanderson nodded to his officers. Get going. Stay on him.

THE INTERROGATION

Inglewood City Hall, California
July 4, 1937

INVESTIGATORS SHADOWED DYER after his strange visit to headquarters and on the Fourth of July, they made their move.

Mid-morning, as the Stephens family was leaving for Jeanette's funeral services, Inglewood Police detectives Williams and Chandler arrived at Dyer's shack on North Commercial Street. They told Dyer they needed to question him about the murder of the three Inglewood girls. Dyer went willingly to the police car, presumably headed for the station.

But first, a few little detours.

They drove to a jungle area close to the city dumps, on Hyde Park near Glenn Way. They parked and worked on Dyer, questioning him again and again. He said nothing until after about ninety minutes, when he finally denied being involved in the crime.

Williams and Chandler turned up the heat a little, asking Dyer to show them where he was on Monday the 28th when he was involved in the search efforts—back to the scene of the crime. Dyer gave them directions to a dirt road off LaBrea, close to the bean field, near the entrance to the ravine. They stopped at the corn stand at Slauson and LaBrea, and Dyer said he was there when he heard about the Boy Scouts finding the bodies.

Then on to the Inglewood jail, where six men were waiting in the main interrogation room. Sheriff Biscailuz, the DA's Investigator Williams, LAPD Lieutenant Sanderson, Sheriff's Captain William

Penprase, and Lieutenants Williams and Chandler. The team got under way at about 3:30 p.m. and questioned Dyer for an hour, but he repeatedly denied having anything to do with the kidnappings and murders.

The investigators decided a change of venue and some additional manpower might help, so officers William and Chandler were instructed to deliver Dyer to the Hall of Justice in Los Angeles, perhaps to remind the suspect that if he continued to be uncooperative there, they would need to bring him back to the Inglewood jail and the seething mob waiting outside.

News that Dyer was being moved quickly reached the Hall of Justice, and reporters and law enforcement officers began swarming. And Mrs. Dyer was in custody on the sixth floor, next to the interrogation room that was readied for Dyer. Once Dyer arrived, officers made sure to walk his wife within Dyer's view before the next round of questioning got under way. It was nearly 8 p.m. when Sanderson and his men resumed their work on the suspect.

It didn't take long to get results. About twenty minutes later, Sanderson emerged to inform reporters that Dyer had confessed.

THE CONFESSIONS

Los Angeles
July 5 and 6, 1937

THE HORROR OF the killer crossing guard was instantly front-page news from coast to coast. A continent away, the *New York Times'* headline "WPA Man Admits Slaying 3 Girls" lured east coast readers into the developing story. Up north in Kalispell, Montana, the *Daily Inter Lake* announced, "Crossing Guard Admits Triple Child Murders." Similar headlines ran in every major newspaper. And concerned listeners around the country sat glued to their radios for the latest reports.

Further, the news assured everyone that the police had found the killer—the only killer. Newspapers recounted the names of other suspects—Dow, Keefe, Godsey and others—whom the police had "absolved" and released. The investigation into other suspects was over. Albert Dyer was the killer.

At the epicenter, the story covered the entire front page of the *Los Angeles Times'* evening edition, with a large picture of Dyer, looking haggard and wrung out after the long session with investigators. And the *Los Angeles Times* promised specifics:

TRIPLE GIRL MURDERS CONFESSED
Crossing Guard Details Crime

The *Los Angeles Times* ran the story using quotes from Dyer's alleged first confession the night before, and the article read like a sensational true crime novel:

> *The three school chums, although they had been warned by their mothers never to venture from the park with a man, left their toys in the park and hiked blithely to the foot of the canyon leading into the Baldwin Hills, where Dyer says he met them shortly after noon.*
>
> *"We entered the canyon from the north end," Dyer rasped with parched throat and lips in his confession.*
>
> *"I choked them with my hands," almost shouted the confessor, clasping his drawn face in his hands, which little more than a week ago had served as garrotes. "Then I put the rope around her neck."*

The details came fast and furious, but fragmented that first day, so reporters and the public were left wanting more. District Attorney Fitts answered the call by releasing portions of Dyer's July 5 confession. The confession from July 5 was reported as Dyer's second, but it was the first that was recorded by a stenographer. The DA titillated by noting he couldn't release the entire confession because he was anticipating a court battle, but he gave the people plenty of what they wanted with excerpts from D.A. Fitts's interrogation session with Dyer. The *Los Angeles Times* headlined it as the "Slayer's Own Story of Inglewood Crime:"

"After you saw that girl swimming, you saw Madeline, Marie and Jeanette and you talked to them?"

"Yes, sir."

"You do string tricks, don't you?"

"Yes, sir."

"Did you do string tricks for these three children Saturday morning in the park?"

"Yes, sir."

"Did you have a book, a Mickey Mouse book, with you at that time?"

"That was the children's."

"Which one had the book?"

"I judge Madeline had the book."

"Just about when did you speak to them Albert—to those little girls about going rabbit hunting?"

"That was Saturday morning."

"About what time? How long had you been in the park?"

"I would judge about two or three hours."

"What did you say to them?"

"I asked them if they wanted to go rabbit hunting."

"Whom did you ask?"

"Madeline, Marie, and Jeanette"

"What did they say?"

"They said they would."

"They knew you very well, didn't they?"

"Yes."

"And when they said they would, you went almost immediately, didn't you?"

"Yes."

"You went first?"

"Yes, sir."

"And the three kids came out of the park and followed you?"

"Yes, sir."

"How far ahead of the children were you?"

"Not so very far, a block I guess."

"You kept watching to see if they followed you?"

"Yes."

"You didn't want everyone to see you with the kids, is that the idea?"

"That's right, yes, sir."

"Now when you started from the park you weren't going to hunt rabbits were you?"

"No, sir."

"What were you taking the children to the hills for?"

"To molest them and attack them."

"You know this canyon where the children were found dead?"

"Yes."

"Did you take them into that canyon where they were found dead?"

"Yes, sir."

"You went in across the bean field?"

"Yes, sir."

"When you came to the barbed wire fence at the head of the bean field how did you get past?"

"I crawled under and held the wire up for the children to crawl under."

"Now, Albert, when you helped the children under the fence you took them down the canyon?"

"Yes."

"All three together?"

"Yes, sir."

"When you got them down there all three together what did you say?"

"I said I would take Madeline first."

"What for?"

"And place her where there was some rabbits."

"And did you leave the other two?"

"Yes, sir."

"What did you intend to do?"

"Strangle her."

"When you got Madeline away from the other two what did you do to her?"

"I strangled her with a rope."

"Did you tie the rope around her neck?"

"Yes, sir."

"Front or back?"

"Back."

"When you strangled her did you make sure she was dead?"

"I said 'Madeline,' and she didn't answer."

"Did you give her any warning before you grabbed her and strangled her?"

"No warning at all. I just grabbed her."

"Then you laid her down or did she fall down?"

"Fell."

"Then what did you do?"

"I went back to the other two girls."

"What did you say?"

"'I got Madeline placed down here.' I said I had placed her where she could catch the rabbits if they would run down."

"And did you stay with the other two?"

"I took one of them."

"Which one did you take?"

"Marie."

"What did you do with Jeanette when you took Marie? Where did you leave Jeanette?"

"Just a few steps from where she was standing."

"You hadn't killed her yet?"

"No."

"When you took Marie down what did you do?"

"I strangled her."

"How did you strangle her?"

"Rope."

"Did Marie struggle at all?"

"Yes, sir, she cried."

"Did she say anything at all?"

"She just said 'Please don't.' I didn't pay no attention, just strangled her."

"Then after you killed her, what did you do?"

"I went back to Jeanette."

"What did you do?"

"I grabbed her and strangled her right off."

"Right where she was?"

"Yes."

"With rope?"

"Yes, sir."

"Did she struggle at all or say anything?"

"No, sir."

"Where did you get the rope?"

"I had it home in the garage."

"Did you put it in your pocket that morning?"

"Yes, sir."

"Let me show you a piece of rope."

"(Throwing both arms in the air and crying) That's Jeanette's!"

"How do you know it's Jeanette's—the hair on it?" (indicating blonde hair in the knot)

"Yes, sir."

[Interrogator's note: I am showing Mr. Dyer a piece of rope taken from the body of Jeanette Stephens and marked by a tag and on this tag is a notation: "Taken from the body of Jeanette Stephens by the Coroner's office."]

"And when you put the rope around the necks of these three children you intended to kill them?"

"Yes, sir."

"What did you do before you left the canyon?"

"When I got done then I knelt down to each one, one by one, and prayed."

"What did you say?"

"I said 'O Lord, forgive my sins and what I have done.'"

"What did you do next?"

"I took their shoes off."

"What did you do with them?"

"I placed them, each little pair together. Laid Madeline's shoes together, Marie's shoes together, and Jeanette's shoes together."

MANY MOMENTS DURING my research are hard to forget—when I first saw the *Los Angeles Times* headline about the missing girls, with my grandparents' names in print, when I first saw the photographs of my family from the Los Angeles Public Library, and when I first read all the reports that Albert Dyer was the confessed killer, no doubt about it, forever remembered as the "Smiling Monster of Inglewood." My family's story was always becoming clearer and more real.

Then I read Dyer's confession and the one sure thing became less certain. I wondered aloud one day, "did they get the wrong man?"

Confessions are the most powerful evidence in any courtroom, and jurors—indeed, most of us—cannot comprehend how someone can confess to something they didn't do. As Justice White of the US Supreme Court wrote in 1968, "A confession is like no other evidence. Indeed, the defendant's own confession is probably the most probative and damaging evidence that can be admitted against him . . . Confessions have profound impact on the jury, so much so that we may justifiably doubt its ability to put them out of mind even if told to do so." In some cases, confessions will overcome overwhelming evidence of innocence such as eyewitness identifications and forensic evidence, even DNA.

Yet more than a quarter of the documented wrongful convictions overturned by DNA evidence in the United States have involved false confessions, usually resulting from questionable interrogations. The continuum spans from the seemingly benign practice of the interrogator telling the story and the suspect merely agreeing just to make the process end, as Dyer may have done to avoid being taken back to the Inglewood mob, to the more worrisome and perfectly legal practice of police lying to suspects about evidence they have against them, and finally to the extreme of physical and psychological abuse.

And false confessions usually happen in precisely the circumstances I was finding in the Dyer case—a police force and community desperate to bring a killer to justice, an apparently mentally challenged suspect, and a team of investigators threatening death, either sooner at the hands of the Inglewood lynch mob or later through imposition of the death penalty.

He's just answering their yes/no questions, I said to myself. Those types of questions allow the interrogators to write the story. They provide the narrative in sentences framed as questions, but for which there is only a yes or no answer, rather than asking open-ended questions and allowing the suspect to provide the facts and the time line. Dyer, like many suspects facing these types of interrogations, sounds like a scared child telling them what they want to hear. He knew where the bodies were because he was there after they were found. He knew the ropes were tied at the backs of the girls' necks because he saw their bodies in the ravine. He knew about the little shoes because they were lined up next to the bodies. And all these facts were endlessly playing out in newspapers and radio for days before he confessed.

What about parts of the confession the *Times* ran the day before that were totally inconsistent with this version of the "slayer's story"? In the first version, Dyer said of Madeline, "I choked her with my hands," and he said he used binding twine, but in the next version, he said he used rope to choke her, and he referred only to clothesline rope. He said he'd only done rope tricks for the girls one time, on that Saturday, but later he said he did it more often. And most conspicuously, he first said he killed Madeline, Jeanette, and then Marie, but then it was Madeline, Marie, and Jeanette. Inconsistencies like these are cause for concern, especially when a suspect is alone with interrogators as Dyer was.

The landmark US Supreme Court decision in *Miranda v. Arizona* requiring officers to read a suspect his rights and allow him to consult an attorney didn't come along for another thirty years, so Dyer was alone for the entire ten-hour process, including the two-hour interrogation in a squad car, the ride to the police station, and the undocumented three hours between the Inglewood police station and the evening interrogation in Los Angeles. Today, the police tactic of driving Dyer by the scene of the crime after the squad-car questioning would arguably trigger the obligation to read him the Miranda warning because that police action is specifically designed to get someone talking while in police custody.

Ironically, if Dyer was innocent, he would have likely declined a lawyer anyway. People who are later proven actually innocent usually do because, the counterintuitive thinking goes, they know they're innocent, so why would they need a lawyer? This is all a big mistake. I'll just answer some questions and be home in time for dinner.

But Dyer received no warnings and he was on his own with interrogators until he gave them what they wanted.

And fairly quickly after he first confessed, he was thrust into the spotlight, with cameras flashing and reporters swarming. So he may have made the connection that confessing brought him a kind of reward in the form of media attention. His foster mother Etta Young told reporters from her Redondo Beach home that Albert confessed because "he is insane and a publicity seeker." The reporters saw it first hand, too, and recounted Dyer's antics in their daily dispatches. He was posing for the cameras every chance he got—including an almost comical shot of him while he was being fingerprinted—and talking with reporters, police officers, his guards at the jail, and really anyone who would pay attention. With such a childlike behavior-reward connection, Dyer would have glossed over the serious damage he might have been inflicting just so he could get another chance to tell his sensational story to an audience of hungry listeners.

Through exonerating more than two thousand people in the United States, we know that people confess to crimes they did not commit. Today, we have many more safeguards to protect against false confessions—the Miranda warning, and most importantly, videotaping of interrogations and any resulting confessions. More than twenty states require that police record interrogations, and more than a thousand other law enforcement agencies voluntarily do so, with reformers working to change practices nationwide so every jurisdiction follows suit. But again, Dyer was afforded no such protections, and law enforcement agencies were under enormous pressure to charge someone.

So, when I consider the lack of safeguards, Albert Dyer's apparent mental challenges, and his intense desire for attention, it's difficult to feel fully confident about his confessions. Dyer's confession worried me and I would need more solid evidence before I could ever believe he was the killer. But the police, and the nation, believed they had their man.

IN INGLEWOOD, WORD had spread quickly the night of July 4 that police had a local crossing guard in custody and he was the killer. When Chief

Campbell returned from the DA's office in Los Angeles to Inglewood City Hall late that night, part of the mob was still there demanding to know if Dyer was in the local jail. Campbell feared the men would start hearing rumors and who knows what they might do, so he invited one of the men in to see for himself that Dyer wasn't there. Campbell and his officers were relieved that Dyer had confessed in Los Angeles and not in Inglewood. One officer told the *Los Angeles Times*, "I don't think we could have kept the enraged populace in hand. I think we would have had a lynching on our hands. All plans had been made by the more inflamed members of the townspeople to drag the confessor to Centinela Park and there string him up to the tree from under which he lured his three victims to their horrible deaths."

That night was the last time the mob gathered at Inglewood City Hall, and the next morning all the reporters packed up their operations. For more than a week they'd been camped there, even sleeping on benches inside the police department, but from here on out all the action would be in Los Angeles. The next morning, Inglewood City Hall was deserted.

IT WAS AFTER 2 a.m. on July 5 when police booked Dyer at the Los Angeles County Jail on three counts of first-degree murder. He first admitted killing the girls a little after 8:00 the night before, and after investigators made him run through his story again, they took him—carried him because he collapsed—to a ladies' restroom so several doctors could examine his genitals for signs of trauma that would have surely resulted from the violent sexual assaults.

He was again near collapse when they finally got him to the jail, but an officer held him upright while he was fingerprinted and processed. Newspaper photographers asked to him pose for pictures and he did, including one in which he tied a tiny string noose while standing at the booking window. The *Los Angeles Times* ran the haunting photograph as part of a full-page photo essay.

SHERIFF'S DEPUTIES ESCORTED a bewildered Mrs. Dyer into the booking room to give her a moment with her husband.

"Albert what have they done to you to make you admit this awful thing?" she cried.

Dyer said nothing and instead moved closer to embrace his wife. He smiled as he leaned in to kiss her. As his lips met hers, she turned to the side ever so slightly to avoid him, and she glanced at the newspaper photographer. The *Los Angeles Times* ran that photograph, too. She looked terrified, like a strange man was forcing himself on her.

WHILE DYER WAS confessing the night before, the streets of Inglewood were reported to be "quiet as a country village." Everyone was at Centinela Park celebrating Independence Day. The crowds were just over the fence from Inglewood Park Cemetery where Jeanette Stephens was laid to rest.

THE CROSSING GUARD

Los Angeles County Jail
July 5, 1937

ALBERT DYER WAS born in 1904 in Indian Lake, New York. Like the Everett children years later, he was moved across the country from New York to California when he was four years old. He lived for a few years in North Dakota before coming back to Redondo Beach, California, where the Young family raised him as an informal foster son.

Etta Young told the *Los Angeles Times*, "We never adopted him but we raised him just like our own boy. He never was able to do very much." She called him "Albert the Chickenhearted."

"Why one time I stepped on a nest of baby mice and killed some of them. Albert set up such a wail I thought I would never calm him down. He always cried like a baby every time anything like that got killed."

His foster father, Grant Young, said Albert "always was crazy about women and I always felt there was something wrong with him somewhere."

Dyer quit school when he was fourteen. He made it to only the fourth-grade level and Etta said he just knew he wasn't going to make it any further so he quit. When he was eighteen, he went to barber school in Los Angeles but quit two weeks before finishing the course.

He never had regular work, but in 1936 he got on with the WPA in Inglewood as a laborer and that job lasted several months until October when they assigned him to work as a crossing guard at Sixty-Seventh Street and Chester Avenue, at the north end of Centinela Park. He worked afternoons at North Marlborough and Brett Streets so he could help children across the street when school let out.

By that time, the Everett and Stephens families lived on East Hazel Street, on the west side of the park, and the girls, Marie, Madeline and Jeanette, attended Centinela Elementary School. Dyer would help them, and other children, across busy East Hyde Park Boulevard as they left the school.

By all accounts, he enjoyed his job and was a good crossing guard.

In the late spring of 1937, Dyer learned that the WPA was planning to let the crossing guards go for the summer. He took great pains to scratch out a letter to the US Senator from California, William McAdoo:

> *Honorable Senator, I hereby protest to take off our crossing guards from our community which at present time is kept up by WPA administration. They are a great help to our children for safe crossing. Please do all you can in your power to prevent such action. Hoping and trust you will do your utmost in this matter. Sincerely yours.*

Dyer never mailed the letter, but apparently he didn't need to. On June 26, he was still on duty as a WPA crossing guard, newly assigned to a location on Redondo Boulevard, just outside Centinela Park.

The only thing interesting about Dyer's history was his criminal record—or lack thereof. On July 19, FBI director J. Edgar Hoover dispatched to the DA's office Dyer's history, showing he was arrested in 1926 for burglary in Redondo Beach and picked up three times in Los Angeles in 1927–1928 for vagrancy, for which he served some short jail stints. But he was never investigated or arrested for anything violent or sexual, and nothing in his past suggested preparation for viciously murdering three children.

ABOUT THE SAME time laypeople would have predictably been assuming that Dyer had to be crazy to commit such heinous acts, the District

Attorney and his deputies were getting concerned about the same thing, that maybe Dyer suffered from mental illness and would be incompetent to stand trial. They wasted no time in finding out, capitalizing on their ready access to the defendant before a lawyer was appointed to represent him.

The prosecution hired four psychiatrists to examine Dyer. On July 5, Doctors Charles Decker, Wells Cook, Aaron Rosenoff, and Paul de River—the latter having prepared the criminal profile for police early in the investigation—interviewed Dyer as a group, and then each met with him individually. They quickly agreed that Dyer's IQ was 60, the mental capacity of a nine- or ten-year-old child. Dr. Rosenoff deemed him "feeble minded."

But they found Dyer sane and, more importantly for the prosecution, competent to stand trial.

The DA's investigator Eugene Williams went first in addressing reporters with the news. "Dyer is sane. His intelligence is only slightly below average. He knew what he was doing. He has no hallucinations but is a sadist and a sexual pervert."

District Attorney Fitts shored up Williams's announcement. "These men spent several hours with Dyer, observing his reactions during and after questioning. They are of the collective opinion that he is sane enough to know what he is doing and saying."

The *New York Times,* in their next installment of this fast-moving story about the "Coast Slayer," reported that Dyer was sane—"Prosecution Alienists Find Dyer A Sadist But Aware of Actions." The California papers carried the same findings and the public was entranced for another day with details about the child killer.

ADDING TO THE media frenzy, the press quickly seized on Albert Dyer's wife, Isabelle. Soon after Albert's arrest and booking, she was put in protective custody at the Los Angeles County Jail, and reporters found her there, already defending her husband.

"I have a right to stand by him. He's my husband, ain't he? Al didn't do it. I know he didn't do it," she sobbed.

"We used to quarrel but we always made up again. And he never even talked about other girls. My husband couldn't have done that awful thing!"

The *Los Angeles Times* described the jail-bound wife as a "bedraggled waif who looks like a wizened, red-eyed child." And they recounted the story of her difficult life:

In the twenty-four years she has lived, Isabelle has found little peace.

Her mother died when she was a child 7 years of age in Pope Valley, near Napa.

She quit school when she was in the seventh grade because her father had no money to send her further.

She went to work and hoped to marry the boy she cared for. She was sent to reform school instead.

At 18, she worked as a maid-of-all-work for a San Francisco family, finally left when the drudgery proved too much for her strength,

Then she met Al, in the romantic setting of a picture show on Market Street. She remembered him from her school days in Pope Valley.

Two years ago they were married in Santa Ana.

They hitch-hiked to Inglewood, where Al had friends.

And here they have lived, quite contentedly for the past seven months since Al got a W.P.A. job as a crossing guard.

On Easter Sunday, in the blinding rain, they moved to the little shack where they stayed until Dyer was arrested.

Isabelle told reporters that Albert Dyer was all she had in the world. Her father accused her of "going with boys" and disappeared. Her only brother was gone, too. But Al remained. He married her.

And he worked hard for her, too, selling papers two nights a week on the streets of Inglewood and faithfully bringing home the money to pour into her lap.

"So I could go to a movie," she whispered wistfully, pushing back the lanky brown hair that fell across her tear-stained eyes. "Friday night he brought $1.94"

"And please excuse me crying. It was such a shock."

DOUBTS

Inglewood, California
July 5, 1937

IN THE DAYS following the murders, my grandmother remained under a doctor's care to deal with her shock and pain. Rather unbelievably, but no doubt because of the continuing competition among the crush of reporters covering every side of the story, several area newspapers ran photos of her on July 5 lying on the couch at home, eyes terribly sunken, her features twisted with grief. In one photo, my grandfather is handing her a glass of water because she'd collapsed after hearing the details of Dyer's confession.

Because of these stories and photos, I always imagined her heavily sedated, in and out of twilight sleep, not able to fully comprehend the nightmare going on around her. But her interviews with reporters tell a different story and reveal her to be articulate and thoughtful even in those desperate hours.

And she shared the same doubts I had about Albert Dyer.

She told reporters, "No one in the whole world is more eager to have the guilty man caught than I am. But I can't help wondering if the authorities have the right one. There are so many points where Albert Dyer's story doesn't tally with the facts."

She took issue with the long walk. "I can't see how it would have been possible for my children to walk all that distance from the park to the hills. Madeline was such a little thing . . . she couldn't have made it. And Marie was too smart. She would have smelled a rat and broken away.

"No, they must have been taken in a car, so that they could not get away. I am certain of that. When we went to Los Angeles, they always wanted to be sure that we knew the way back home. They loved it here and nothing could make them leave it."

My grandfather, at his wife's side, nodded in agreement.

The *Los Angeles Times* reporter wrote: "Singularly lacking in hate, the mother of the dead girls yesterday had sympathy for the man who might be falsely accused. 'Think what it will mean to him all his life, even if they find he's innocent.'" Somehow, my grandmother found room in her broken heart for Albert Dyer.

My grandfather didn't believe Dyer's confession, either. He insisted the girls would not have walked so far to the ravine and he observed—way ahead of his time—that "some men will confess anything under pressure, you know, especially if they're a little weak-minded."

My grandparents weren't alone.

Several people who were in the park on Saturday also refused to believe it was Dyer. Haskell Wright, who worked in the park, led the pack in talking to reporters, and he was convincing, having known Dyer for some time.

"Dyer was not with the children either Friday or Saturday," Wright insisted. "I wasn't two feet from the man Friday and Saturday morning. Kenneth Hylander was just as close. We saw the same man and he was not Dyer."

Wright and Hylander also told reporters they'd refused earlier to agree with two women who said they were positive they saw ex-con Luther Dow playing with the girls—so, if anyone thought Wright might be trying to save Dyer because he knew him, Wright's objection to the Dow identification seemed to show that Wright wasn't merely trying to save a friend. He clearly saw someone else, not Dyer, and not Dow.

Twelve-year-old Amy Lancey agreed and told police she saw Fred Godsey in the park on Saturday morning and then again that night and the following day. She said his dungarees were torn and he had scratches on his face.

Even my Aunt Olive stuck by her previous identifications of Godsey as Eddie the Sailor, and she was an especially compelling witness. She knew Dyer as the neighborhood crossing guard, and she'd been in the park the afternoon before when Eddie asked her to go rabbit hunting.

Then there was the curious case of Mr. and Mrs. Fish. The two had once lived with the Dyers and now they were neighbors. Mr. Fish was also a fellow WPA crossing guard. An investigator with the Inglewood Police Department told the *Inglewood Daily News* that he'd found in the incinerator at the Fish home a crossing guard arm band, rope similar to that found around the girls' necks, and a cigar box with what appeared to be blood on it. He also reported that Mr. Fish was one of the crossing guards standing with Albert Dyer when officers drove Mike Huerta by to identify the man he said had been trying to lure boys from the park.

Mrs. Fish told investigators she'd seen Albert Dyer downtown with a moustache the Friday morning before the crime. When she saw him a few hours later, he'd shaved it off, so he couldn't possibly have been the moustached suspect people reported seeing in the park with the girls. But the doubting Inglewood police officers checked reports that one of Dyer's good friends, not Dyer, as Mrs. Fish originally told them, wore a moustache on the day the bodies were found then shaved it off the next day. And people described the friend with the shaved moustache as "hysterical with excitement" the day Dyer confessed.

Authorities held the Fishes as material witnesses in the Los Angeles County Jail for a night after Dyer confessed, although they never explained what information the Fishes may have had or why they required police protection. And the evidence reportedly found in their home never surfaced again in the press or the courtroom.

After so many conflicting accounts, reporters confronted the DA's office and suggested that someone else may have been involved in the crime. Chief Investigator Eugene Williams responded economically and calmly. "There is no evidence that Dyer had any accomplice. This office will ask that he be hanged for committing one of the most horrible crimes in the history of California." No further comments.

AND SO THE stage was set for the dangerous tunnel vision tendency in such cases to home in on a suspect at the expense of exploring others, sometimes referred to as "target lock." As the story plays out so sensationally in the media, and as the community recoils further in fear, the need to catch someone, or to keep a perceived perpetrator in custody, becomes so urgent that police must work more quickly, with little time to fully develop leads and tips. Their desperation also creates a receptivity to information that supports the leading theory or suspect. In turn, investigators will—inadvertently or in some cases, quite intentionally—urge eyewitnesses to confirm that a suspect is the man they saw. And soon, the wheels of justice begin turning in only one direction and the conditions are ripe for mistakes, as they may have been in those early days when Albert Dyer confessed and investigators stopped pursuing any other suspects, including the formerly hunted Fred Godsey.

But I never stopped thinking about Godsey, "Freddie the Sailor," no matter how much of the case I unearthed. And after I read Dyer's alleged confession and first questioned his involvement, Godsey became even more compelling.

I remembered how investigators, shortly after confirming Othel Strong's alibi, learned about Godsey and then circulated Godsey's photo to eyewitnesses, all of whom said he was the man they'd seen talking to the girls. All those people who'd previously identified Strong's photo said no, Godsey is the man. Even my Aunt Olive said yes, he was the man who talked to us on Friday, who wanted to take us rabbit hunting. The man with the disjointed wrists and the rope tricks. And I thought about the leading cause of wrongful convictions —a problem with police investigations that's still with us today.

Eyewitness misidentifications have led to 75 percent of the wrongful convictions overturned by DNA evidence in our country, and many of those mistakes happen early in the process when police are desperately seeking a suspect, just as they were in Inglewood in those frantic days after June 26.

They talk to people who were at the scene—who could be more reliable? What did you see? What did he look like? Which direction was he heading? And soon a picture emerges—an actual mug shot as in the case of Othel Strong or a well-intentioned police sketch—and that image drives everything. But three-quarters of the time, eyewitnesses get it wrong. Maybe they get the broad outlines of the suspect correct, but they cannot identify the actual perpetrator.

Leading researchers have identified several issues that particularly affect identifications in the criminal context. Memory is simply unreliable and it becomes even more so with certain factors like bad lighting, obscured views, distance, unfamiliarity, the presence of a distracting weapon, or with cross-racial identifications. And when people are under pressure—perceived or real—from the police, the media, or other criminal justice players, they want to please, they want to do anything to help, and often that means agreeing with what they believe police are suggesting, or with what they believe everyone is saying. Researchers have also demonstrated how eyewitness memory is compromised dramatically almost immediately after someone sees a person or event, and it continues to deteriorate from there.

And yet, as US Supreme Court Justice William Brennan put it best in a 1981 dissent, "[t]here is almost nothing more convincing to a jury than a live human being who takes the stand, points a finger at the defendant, and says 'That's the one.'"

In fact, my interest in wrongful convictions started with one of the seminal examples of this issue: the Ronald Cotton case. In 1984, college student Jennifer Thompson was raped, but she was able to study her attacker's face, his voice—everything she could observe—in hopes of helping police catch him. She survived, and, based on her information, police developed a composite sketch of the rapist, one that looked very much like Ronald Cotton.

Cotton was innocent and figured the whole thing was just a mistake he could easily correct, so, like many innocent suspects, he went to the police station to clear things up. But he never left.

Thompson identified him in a photo lineup and then in a live lineup. And at trial, she pointed to him from the witness stand—yes, that's the man. Cotton was quickly convicted and sentenced to life in prison.

The real rapist, as later proved by DNA evidence, was a man named Bobby Poole, who looked incredibly like Ronald Cotton. But Jennifer never saw Poole—not in a photo and not in a live lineup. And without Poole in the mix, Ronald Cotton was misidentified because he was the closest thing to what Jennifer remembered. Memory is indeed tricky, but even where we would expect it to be reliable like in Jennifer's case where she studied someone, intent on being able to identify him later, it makes no difference when the actual suspect is not presented because our brains tell us to pick the closest match.

In Inglewood, police interviewed the first witnesses nearly twenty-four hours after the girls left the park, and other witnesses, even later than that. And police were asking people to recall something they casually observed in a busy park setting, rather than something they knew they would need to remember.

Much like the Cotton case, the initial general picture that emerged was fairly consistent—5'10/11" tall, 140–160 lbs., dark hair, dark complexion, moustache, a tattoo, a Ford roadster and all the rest—all descriptions that fit Fred Godsey. But without Godsey's photo available at the outset, people identified Othel Strong and they did so with great conviction. If Othel Strong had no alibi and if police were never tipped about Godsey, Strong would likely have been charged and possibly convicted based on so many eyewitnesses putting him in the park that day. The exoneration annals are filled with such cases where the point of the finger is all it takes.

So, when first I saw Godsey's photo, I thought, *that's him—he's the Bobby Poole of this case.*

I also thought about how the girls, including Olive, knew Dyer well. Family friend June Hazley said they all knew him and called him by name—"Mr. Dyer" or sometimes even "Al." Howard Hilborn remembered him clearly, what he looked like, that he was very short, with a friendly and joking manner, and Howard wasn't even on Dyer's regular route like Olive, Marie, and Madeline. So, when Jeanette Stephens ran to the pool attendant for rope and said she was getting it for Eddie the Sailor, it couldn't have been Dyer who asked for the rope—unless Dyer cleverly started calling himself Eddie or

Freddie the Sailor to force a mistaken identification, but surely he wasn't bright enough for that plan. And the girls certainly wouldn't have misidentified him the day before the murders when they ran home to tell their mom about the stranger who wanted to take them rabbit hunting, nor would all those children who knew him as the crossing guard and placed him in the park Saturday morning.

Godsey also had a car. Recall the men who said Godsey sold them a goat earlier that morning, secured in a 1929 or 1930 fenderless Ford by a length of clothesline, and two other men who said they saw a man who looked like Godsey with three little girls in the same type of Ford that morning in front of the park. Lillian Popp, who also knew Dyer, almost went with the girls and was close enough to identify Godsey and the car. Olive testified specifically that the man who asked her to go rabbit hunting on Friday said he had a car. Dyer did not.

And what about the disjointed wrists? Multiple children do not fabricate that kind of distinguishing fact. Little Amy Lancey reported the wrists, too, and said she saw Godsey displaying the trick in the park Saturday morning. Dyer was never reported to have, and never demonstrated, any such ability. The *Inglewood Daily News*, reporting on Godsey as a nonsuspect after Dyer's confession, noted that "The present suspect [Dyer] has no car. He does, however, have some tattooing on his arms but so far as known, he does no rope tricks and has no unusually supple wrist joints, such as have been reported as characteristics of the man who lured the little girls to their terrible doom."

The man who talked to Olive on Friday also told her he had a wife and a daughter, and Godsey was indeed married with a young daughter back in Utah. Dyer was married but had no children.

I came back often in my mind to an exclusive article the *Los Angeles Times* published on July 4 while Godsey was being hunted. A man who knew Godsey, but who would only go on record as John Doe because he so feared Godsey, wrote that Godsey was the most cruel person he'd ever known. He described how Godsey once got in a bar fight and chewed off his opponent's ear. "Pain and suffering inflicted on others meant absolutely nothing to him," while Albert

Dyer's foster mother described how he once cried when she stepped on some baby mice.

Godsey's friend also confirmed a long history of Godsey molesting young girls in the places he worked and lived, always getting fired and having to move on. He mentioned how he could flip his wrists back onto his forearms and that he had superhuman strength, tearing phone books in two to demonstrate his powerful hands and arms. And most chilling, the man described how Godsey could endear himself to children with stories and rope tricks, luring them in, wide-eyed and enchanted. When I read that about Godsey, all I could see were my aunts and Jeanette running by Mrs. Craycroft that morning, singing merrily about their rabbit hunt.

I have such a strong feeling about Godsey.

It's entirely plausible that Godsey committed the murders alone and slipped away while the authorities homed in on Albert Dyer. And Dyer's narcissism and self-aggrandizing nature, along with a little police coercion, could have compelled him to take full credit for the crime while Godsey faded into oblivion.

At the very least, Godsey could have been the main actor, with Dyer as an accomplice, intentional or otherwise. Perhaps Godsey enlisted Dyer to make the girls feel safe with someone they recognized and then to walk them to the ravine so Godsey could cut off the connection to them in his car, as eyewitnesses saw earlier that morning. One can imagine Dyer taking, or at least not understanding, that bait.

Godsey's apparent presence in the park and his unique features are all the more troublesome because I simply can't imagine Dyer pulling off the crime alone, or at all. How could Dyer, with his nine-year-old illiterate mind and scattered thinking, act so methodically and efficiently to murder three children in what were surely moments of frantic anticipation? It seems plausible that he may have had, or even needed, an accomplice. Why didn't Marie, who was the oldest and who would have, in my grandmother's words, "smelled a rat," act or flee when her sister and Jeanette were taken away? Did someone else hold her there? And if there was someone else, perhaps in Dyer's challenged mind, the desire for publicity and a singular spotlight would be more important to him than being blamed for something he didn't do.

But again, because Dyer confessed, Godsey was abandoned as a suspect. The *Inglewood Daily News* included Godsey in a summary of "Hot Suspects Absolved," noting he'd been "blasted in the metropolitan press as a murderous individual and for whom a search throughout the Southwest was instituted." The head detective for the Salt Lake City Police Department told reporters that as soon as Albert Dyer confessed, the Los Angeles authorities instructed his department to call off the search for Godsey. "We have received no order to begin looking for him again." So, the trail went cold and the Los Angeles press stopped reporting on Godsey altogether.

Meanwhile, he continued to commit crimes. An Iowa newspaper reported in 1947 that he'd been arrested for intoxication in the town of Corning and while he was serving a short jail sentence there, the local authorities sent his fingerprints to the FBI. The results came in after Godsey was released, and the sheriff was surprised to learn about a rather lengthy criminal history—fifty-two entries with crimes including forgery, assault, burglary, larceny and "indecent liberties with a child." Since 1930, he'd been arrested in fourteen states, including California, and remarkably, he was arrested again in Greenfield, Iowa, just shortly after the Corning incident.

Godsey died sometime between the Iowa incidents and 1949, but the specifics seem to be lost to the sands of time or to the deliberate efforts of a man who laid low while someone else answered to triple murder charges. In the end, he may have played a role in the deaths or he may have just been terrified of getting caught up in the whole mess.

AS THE DA'S office focused on confessed killer Albert Dyer, Haskell Wright pressed on, claiming around town, to anyone and any reporter who would listen, that Dyer was not the killer.

The DA's office quickly reached its limit with Wright.

Investigator Williams publicly invited Wright and the press to his office. When Wright said he knew at least five men who saw Dyer Saturday afternoon during the time of the alleged crime, Williams asked him to name the men. When Wright refused, Williams escorted him, with reporters watching, to the Los Angeles County Public Defender's office.

"After all," Williams quipped, "if Mr. Wright has such information, he should give it to the authorities." *Put up or shut up*, Williams seemed to say.

MAKING SURE

Office of the District Attorney, Los Angeles, California
July 5, 1937

DESPITE THE SCATTERED doubts and many unanswered questions, the wheels of justice were turning and District Attorney Buron Fitts was determined to keep things moving, with everything going by the book. Or at least, it would appear to be going by the book.

Fitts told reporters that he'd brought Dyer into his office at 9:00 a.m. and, along with Sheriff Biscailuz, told Dyer that if his confessions from the night before were untrue, this was his chance to set the record straight.

"If you've been mistreated or abused in any way and forced to make the confession you did, we want you to retract your admission of guilt and you will be afforded every protection."

Dyer allegedly raised his right hand and said, "Before God, I swear I killed those three children and attacked them."

And then, according to Fitts, Dyer proceeded to recount the crime again in horrifying detail.

Newspapers ran the story everywhere.

GIVING DYER SUCH a clear and public chance to recant his confession was interesting, and it was similar to Lieutenant Sanderson telling Dyer's wife post-confession that "there's not a mark on him." Fitts knew the public—and Dyer's eventual defense attorneys—would raise the issue of coercion and it would be much harder to refute those claims weeks or months later. It made sense. Let's get it on the record now and the prosecution would be nearly bulletproof on the point later.

But there is no such record.

On the contrary, with a stenographer poised and ready at the Hall of Justice to record what would be Dyer's second full confession, Fitts and Biscailuz instead met with Dyer in a private office. Then later, with the stenographer present, they questioned him about the private meeting.

"Albert, I want you to take your time, think as long as you want to and as accurately in whatever story you tell as you can be. Before I started to take this statement, you had a little talk with Sheriff Biscailuz and myself personally, didn't you?"

"Yes, sir."

"And the Sheriff and I told you who we were, didn't we?"

"Yes, sir."

"And we told you that whatever story or statement you made would be made voluntarily and freely on your part, didn't we?"

"Yes, sir."

"That you didn't have to tell us anything?"

"Yes, sir."

"We told you that if you had any idea that you had to talk or that we would force you, that that was wrong, didn't we?"

"Yes, sir."

"We told you that by all means if you didn't kill these children and rape them, you ought to tell the Sheriff and myself, didn't we?"

"Yes, sir."

"We told you likewise that we wanted your correct story just as you remember the story, didn't we?"

"Yes, sir."

"And, therefore, when you told Sheriff Biscailuz and myself that the story that you told last night was substantially true . . .?"

"Yes, sir."

"That you had killed and raped these children, you told us that again this morning after we made the statement to you that I have just repeated, didn't you?"

"Yes, sir."

"And that is true, isn't it?"

"Yes, sir."

"Therefore, everything you have said this morning and everything you will say will be freely said by you, voluntarily said, won't it?"

"You ask the questions and I'll answer."

"You will tell it freely. We are not making you do it?"

"Yes, sir."

"We are not compelling you to do it?"

"Yes, sir."

"We are not threatening you if you don't do it, you understand?"

"Yes, sir."

"Notwithstanding, you want to tell the story, don't you?"

"Yes, sir."

Fifteen yes-or-no questions and Albert Dyer agreed with every one of them. Another police-provided script for Dyer to follow.

And when the questioning really began, Dyer went off script easily and often.

The Friday before the kidnappings, he'd left work and gotten home about noon and then went uptown from 2 p.m. to 4 p.m. Then he went home for the night.

"Did you sell papers that evening?"

"Yes, I sold papers Friday night."

"You got home about 4?"

"Then I went back and sold papers."

"About how long did you sell papers?"

"I didn't get home until about 11."

"What time did you start to begin selling papers?"

"The time, I waited around there until about 9 o'clock before the extra came out."

"About what?"

"It said 'Woman Suspect Inglewood Killings.'"

"Wait a minute. This is Friday, the day before you took them from the park. I am talking about the day before, not Saturday."

"I didn't go over in the park Friday."

HE WENT TO the park Saturday morning at 10 a.m. He saw the girls by the swimming pool.

"What girls?"

"The Everett and Jeanette Stephens."

"Name the Everett girls."

"Marie and Madeline, and Jeanette."

"Jeanette Stephens?"

"Yes, sir."

"You didn't see Olive?"

"Yes, sir."

"Was she there that morning?"

"Yes, sir."

"Are you sure about that?"

"Yes, sir."

"This is Saturday morning when you took the children?"

"Yes, sir."

"You are sure she was over there?"

"Yes, sir."

"Just forget you have ever made any statement to us and don't refer to last night, but tell us this morning as if you were telling it the first time. You saw little Olive, Marie, and Madeline Everett in the park Saturday morning?"

"Yes, sir."

"Are you sure you saw Olive at the park on Saturday morning?"

"No."

"As a matter of fact, you didn't see her that morning, did you?"

"No."

WHEN ASKED IF he knew people who worked in the park, Dyer mentions Haskell Wright. Fitts asks what Wright looked like, what size?

"He is pretty tall. He said he saw Eddie the Sailor."

But Fitts doesn't follow up. He goes on to the next question about whether Dyer talked to anyone in the park that morning other than the girls.

THE REST OF the statement is equally perplexing. Dyer had scouted out the ravine a month earlier. He met the girls at the corn stand instead of the bean field entrance. The children agreed to meet him at the entrance and he didn't really walk with them, but quite some distance ahead of them. He also claimed that he strangled the girls with the ropes and not with his hands as he'd confessed earlier. He'd grabbed them with his hands to keep them from screaming but he used the ropes to kill them. He took Madeline up the canyon first, then Marie up the canyon, too. "Up, no, down." And when he seems confused, Fitts guides him by asking if he took the body down the canyon.

Yes, sir.

DYER ALSO MENTIONED another crossing guard who worked in the same area near the park with Dyer—a man named "Eddie." He was a bigger man, with a moustache, dark complexion. He was working on Friday, June 25. Dyer remembered Eddie was wearing his crossing guard cap.

LATER THAT DAY rumors circulated that Dyer was bargaining, begging Fitts to allow him to plead guilty in exchange for life in prison, rather than the death penalty. Fitts quickly put an end to those rumors at a hastily called press conference.

"This case goes to the grand jury tomorrow. I will ask for a first-degree murder indictment. A quick trial will be required. The death penalty will be demanded."

BACK AT THE Los Angeles County Jail, Isabelle Dyer was now telling her interrogators that her husband was gone from 11 a.m. until 6 p.m. on the day of the murders. She sobbed her answers.

"I haven't any idea where he was. All I know is that he came home all tired out."

But she refused to believe he was guilty.

She told police that Dyer asked her to start a scrapbook about the missing girls, you know, newspaper clippings and things about the case. He'd known all three of the little girls and it was so terribly sad. She remembered how one day she went out to the crossing where he worked and he pointed out some children to her, some little girls, she seemed to recall. "Ain't they cute children?" he asked. She wondered if those were the girls who'd been killed.

She'd arranged the stories in a loose-leaf notebook and labeled the front "Marge." She planned to write magazine stories about the murders one day.

WHILE ISABELLE MAINTAINED her husband was innocent, officers were moving Dyer to the "high power" tank at the Los Angeles County Jail, where serious offenders were kept in solitary cells under constant watch. His close neighbors included the "Rattlesnake Killer," Robert James, who took out an insurance policy on his wife and then tried to kill her with rattlesnakes, but ultimately resorted to drowning her instead, and "the Revelator," John Hunt, disciple of Father Divine, who was later convicted of illegally transporting a minor across state lines for immoral purposes when he took seventeen-year-old Delight Jewett from Colorado to California, renamed her the Virgin Mary, and began having sexual relations with her so she could give birth to "the New Redeemer."

The motley tank crew taunted Dyer as guards took him to his cell, but he cast his bloodshot eyes downward and shuffled along. Jail officials put Dyer on twenty-four-hour suicide watch, rotating teams of guards every three hours. A lightbulb burned all day and night in his cell. He was not allowed to see any newspapers. There were too many stories about how the district attorney was going to hang him.

AS EVENTS UNFOLDED fast and furiously in Los Angeles, my grandparents seemed to be considering that Albert Dyer might be the man who killed their little girls after all. Merle Everett talked to reporters the night of July 5, after Dyer detailed his crime for investigators a second time earlier that day.

"We were told first that Melba and Madeline had made an appointment to meet this man in the hills. My wife and I knew that our children would not go that distance to keep an appointment. But it is quite possible that they would follow someone they trusted."

Their minds must have been reeling remembering all the times the crossing guard had walked the girls home.

THE GRAND JURY

Hall of Justice, Los Angeles, California
July 6, 1937

A *LOS ANGELES TIMES* reporter aptly identified the grand jury proceedings in the Dyer case as the "first step in the legal ladder on which the State hopes to send Albert Dyer to the gallows for the murder of three Inglewood schoolgirls." The grand jury would have to find probable cause to believe that Dyer committed the murders—not that he was the killer beyond a reasonable doubt, as would be the task of a jury to decide at trial. The grand jury was tasked with determining only if there was enough for the case to go forward.

The DA's office called a special session and the grand jury assembled at 8:00 that night, just forty-eight hours after Dyer's alleged first confession. Twenty deputies with the Los Angeles County Sheriff stood guard in the hallways between the grand jury courtroom and the elevator that linked the courthouse with the jail, on alert for anyone who might want to take the law into their own hands. Officers eventually emerged from the elevator with Dyer and took him to a hallway near the courtroom. DA Fitts came out of the courtroom to get Dyer, and Fitts said that, as the two walked back together, Fitts counseled the accused killer.

"Albert, yesterday the Sheriff and I asked you, as the two heads of the department, to tell us whether you did this job or not; you told us that you did and I then took your statement. Now then, I am taking you before the most completely independent tribunal or body in Los Angeles County, the Grand Jury; there are nineteen of them in there;

this jury will protect you; if you did not do it, you tell them; if you did do it you tell them; you tell them exactly as well as you can remember what happened; take your time and be sure you are right in what you say; tell your story as you remember it, whatever that story is. Will you do that?"

Fitts said Dyer replied, "I will."

They finally entered the courtroom, Fitts turned Dyer over to the bailiff and began addressing the grand jury, outlining Dyer's confession of July 4 and his confirmation of that confession the next day on July 5.

Then Dyer took the stand and prepared to confess again.

But he still didn't have an attorney so Fitts, despite the obvious conflict of interest and in direct contravention of his informal counseling outside the courtroom about how this jury would protect Dyer, warned the accused that he did not have to testify and that doing so could result in him having to stand trial for the alleged crimes. Fitts also referred to the prior confessions and asked Dyer to confirm that "before you made these statements to the officers and to myself yesterday, and all the officers, everybody treated you kindly?"

"Yes, sir."

"There never has been any force used upon you?"

"No, sir."

"Nobody had hit you, or anything of that sort, had they? None of the officers had hit you?"

Dyer hesitated, "I am going to ask you, do you remember when that one kind of slapped me?"

"Which one was that?"

"I don't know which one. Plain suit fellow."

"In my presence?"

"Yes, you were there when the rest of them—"

"No, no officer slapped you in my presence. You know that. Do you know what officer it was?"

"No, I don't."

And that was that. Fitts moved on, recounting the friendly meeting with him and Biscailuz that morning, and Dyer began another endless string of "yes, sir" responses, including one in which he effectively gave up his Fifth Amendment protection against self-incrimination. Fitts began a new round of questioning, and Dyer confessed again, answering the questions but with more inconsistencies—saying they left the park at 2, they went to the "Malden Hills," the gate had four strings of barbed wire, and confusing again the order in which he killed and raped the girls. But Fitts clarifies each time and eventually Dyer answers correctly.

"Yes, sir."

THE ONLY OTHER people called to testify that night were a sheriff's deputy who'd been at the ravine, the autopsy surgeon, and one parent of each of the murdered girls. Floyd Stephens heroically answered the prosecutor's few questions regarding Jeanette, and then my grandmother's brother, Don Oliver, spoke for the Everetts. Both men had to look at the morgue photos and confirm that *yes, those are the girls.*

IT TOOK LESS than two hours for the grand jury to return their indictment to Superior Court Judge Thomas Ambrose, and around midnight he ordered Albert Dyer to stand before him while the judge read the indictment on three counts of first-degree murder. No one, not even Dyer, seemed very surprised by what was happening.

The judge then called for the arraignment to begin so Dyer could plead guilty on the record. But DA Fitts said he didn't want Dyer to enter a plea because Dyer didn't have a lawyer yet, and the judge agreed.

"Have you any idea, Mr. Dyer, when you will make arrangements for representation?"

"Your Honor, Judge, I plead guilty!!"

Judge Ambrose probably felt that terrible pain that any officer of the court feels when a defendant who is almost certainly guilty does everything possible to hasten his own conviction. As much as Ambrose and everyone else wanted to see the person who murdered those poor children pay for their crime, he could not have wanted it to happen like this, not in a courtroom operating under the rule of law.

Ambrose appointed public defender Frederic Vercoe for Dyer and continued the arraignment until 9:30 a.m. on the 8th.

DA Fitts began to address the judge about a few other issues when Dyer suddenly fainted and fell to the floor. Judge Ambrose called for order to quiet the chamber while sheriff's deputies carried the unconscious Dyer out of the court and back to his jail cell.

Outside, a bit later, private attorney Peter Rice announced to reporters—within earshot of DA Fitts, who was leaving the building—that some of Dyer's friends were asking him to defend Dyer. Fitts stopped.

"I'm glad to hear that," he said. "My office wants this man to have the best legal advice he can get because we're going to hang him."

ISABELLE DYER WAS starting to crack. She'd been in protective custody at the Los Angeles County Jail for two nights since Albert first confessed. It must have reminded her of when she was held at the Sonoma State Home, a psychiatric facility. She'd escaped from there several years earlier, and the police would eventually find out and send her back. The walls were closing in, and her story was ever-changing.

"My husband said he was sorry for those children before their bodies were found."

She told the police officers how Albert wanted her to go into the hills with him and join the search, and how he'd taken her to the Baldwin Hills two years earlier to see the city lights.

"But Mrs. Dyer, you told us earlier that he took you into the hills just recently."

"Is he trying to implicate me in this thing?" she sobbed. "I couldn't do a thing like that. I am telling you the truth!"

But much like her husband's, her mood changed without warning and the *Los Angeles Times* reported that she "brightened as cameramen continued to take her picture."

"Gee, I'm sure getting tired of having my picture taken. You know, I've never had my picture taken before this happened."

Then, contrary to her earlier statements to reporters, she denied that she ever knew Dyer before she met him in the San Francisco movie house.

The *Times* reported that she was hysterical and sobbing for most of the interview.

THE ONLY PERSON more out of touch with reality was Albert. The next day at the jail, he met with his newly appointed attorney and then reporters, telling them, "I hope I get probation so that I can go back to my wife and get a good job and buy her some pretty things."

As the case rolled on, his hunger for media attention seemed to intensify. He posed for pictures, smiling, performing like a trained seal for the photographers. One of his jailers quipped to a reporter as Dyer was holding court, flashbulbs popping left and right, "That guy will stand on his head for you if you ask him."

THE CRIMINAL MIND

Los Angeles County Jail, California
July 7 and 8, 1937

WITH THE GRAND jury's indictment in hand, DA Fitts wanted another psychiatrist to examine the defendant, just to be sure that Dyer was sane. When Dr. Samuel Marcus arrived at Dyer's jail cell on July 7, Dyer was again posing for newspaper photographers. As Marcus got started, reporters documented the exchange.

"I've been appointed to find out how you're getting along Dyer."

"Oh, I'm all right, except that I have dizzy spells."

"What causes them?" Dr. Marcus asked.

"A couple of years ago near my house, someone hit me on the head and I've been having them ever since. I had one last night but I had a good sleep and feel fine today."

When Marcus asked Dyer how long he'd been a crossing guard, Dyer told him "about a year."

"What would you like to do now," Marcus probed further.

"All I want is to go back to my wife and get a good steady job and show the people I'm all right."

"Don't you want to go back to the crossing guard job?"

"No, I can't support my wife on $55 a month. I don't want that job again."

Just a short time later when Marcus asked Dyer why he'd killed and ravaged the three girls, Dyer said he'd wanted to have sex with women who were younger than his wife. "She's 24 but she looks 10 years older."

A COUPLE OF hours later, court-appointed psychiatrists for the defense arrived at the jail. Sheriff's deputies led Dyer into an interrogation room to meet with the doctors. Dyer immediately admitted that he killed the girls.

But the doctors weren't satisfied and they went back the next day. Same room. Dyer was led in. And he immediately told the doctors he didn't do it. Then he admitted it again. And then he denied it again.

"I didn't do it."

"But you have already confessed that you did do it," defense psychiatrist Dr. Worley explained, trying to hide how exasperated he was.

"I told the others that story, but I didn't do it."

"Why did you confess if you didn't do it?"

"I thought I might as well say I did it when I didn't."

"Why are you denying it now?"

"When the officers told me I would hang for what I did I made up my mind I would say I did not do it."

But Dyer went on.

"I think I was crazy. I did it all just for sexual passion. That was so great on me I had no control. I think it was so great that it amounted to insanity."

Dr. Worley wrote later in his report: "The defendant is very unemotional and does not seem to realize the gravity of the situation in which he has precipitated himself. He felt he would possibly get two years in the penitentiary and then get paroled. Since being told he would hang or get life, he is now more fearful but still lacks emotion."

THE PROSECUTION'S PSYCHIATRIST, Dr. Marcus, also came back that next day and examined Dyer:

Marcus: What is the capital of the United States?
Albert Dyer: Washington
M: What is the capital of California?
D: Sacramento
M: What is the largest river in the United States?

D: Hudson

M: Name some previous presidents

D: I don't know

M: What country is south of the United States?

D: Alaska

M: What is the difference between ice and water?

D: Ice is hard and water is soft

M: Make a sentence of the three words: pen, ink and paper

D: I can use my pen, ink and paper

M: What is the difference between a lie and a mistake?

D: A lie is when you are not telling the truth and a mistake is when you are making a mistake

M: Seven times six equals what?

D: 42

M: Nine times nine?

D: 18

M: Name the days of the week?

D: Sunday, Saturday, Thursday, Friday

Eyelash: Something that lays on your eye

Haste: When you don't like somebody

Mars: If you mars something

Peculiarity: To love anyone

Priceless: When you got no pride

Disproportionate: Passionate or something like that

Shrewd: When a fellow is wrong and mean

Lotus: If anybody is crazy

Bewail: If anybody is well

Flaunt: Don't know

Philanthropy: If you give anything

Ochre: If you shock anybody or strangle anybody

REPORTERS TRACKED DOWN Dyer's foster father, Grant Young, in Merced, California.

"It came as a terrible shock to me when I first saw his picture in the paper. I went down the street crying. It was such a terrible thing.

But I'm not going to take any action. I have had nothing to do with him since he was 19 years old."

AFTER ALL THE examinations, even the defense doctors agreed that Albert Dyer was legally sane. In 1937, California followed the M'Naghten Rule, which applies a "right-wrong" test to determine insanity. Specifically, the rule requires a finding that at the time of the crime, the accused was laboring under such a defect of reason, from disease of the mind, that he did not know the nature and quality of the act he was doing, or if he did know it, that he did not know what he was doing was wrong.

So, despite his confused and illiterate answers to many questions, Dyer was sane under the law because he was not diagnosed with any mental disease and, based on his confessions and other comments about planning the crime and fearing punishment, he knew what he was doing when he killed the girls and he knew that his acts were criminal. It made sense that attorneys in Fred Vercoe's office didn't spend a lot of time on this issue. No, an insanity defense would surely fail and they would have to decide soon how Dyer would plead at the arraignment.

MY CONCERNS ABOUT Dyer's confessions never waned, but I back-burnered them to keep an open mind about the rest of the evidence. Then I read the results of his psychiatric tests and those concerns deepened.

I thought of the tragic case of Earl "Junior" Washington, wrongfully convicted of rape in Virginia in 1984 when he was twenty years old. He was sentenced to death and served seventeen years in prison—at one point coming within nine days of his scheduled execution date—but was exonerated through DNA evidence. Like Dyer, Washington had the mental aptitude of a ten-year-old. Also like Dyer, who only made it to the fourth grade, Washington struggled in school and his third-grade teacher wrote that the boy had "about reached his ability." A psychologist reported that Washington couldn't tell him the colors of the American flag or explain the purpose of a thermometer. He also could not define elementary terms like "fabric," "repair," or "assemble," just as Dyer was unable to define the simple words in his test, like "haste," "priceless," and "eyelash."

And most disturbing, Earl Washington's confession read much like Dyer's.

Did you commit the break-in down the street?

"Yes, sir."

Did you do the burglary on Winchester Street?

"Yes, sir."

Did you rape a woman in town?

"Yes, sir."

Earl Washington confessed to every crime the police mentioned but, like Dyer, he was inconsistent with details, sometimes adding conflicting facts, sometimes changing his story. I thought of Washington every time I read Albert Dyer's confessions. "Yes, sir." "No, sir."

I also thought about my grandfather. "Some men will confess to anything, especially if they're a little weak-minded." Yes, exactly.

Years ago, before I'd learned about wrongful convictions, I wouldn't have thought twice about some of these wrinkles in the case—so what if Dyer can't get every detail straight, he's mentally challenged but clearly he's confessing, and so it goes.

But here I was finding textbook issues in a decades-old story, and like so many of these cases, I was also finding damning evidence. And that's what's so perilous about criminal investigations and prosecutions. Many times the evidence can seem overwhelming or conclusive on the front end because we're looking at it in ways that support our—sometimes desperately held—views that we have the right man.

Of course, DNA testing would have answered all our questions. If Albert Dyer was indeed the killer, one cheek swab would have meant case closed, almost immediately. And if Eddie or Freddie the Sailor had been previously convicted of a qualifying felony, his DNA would come up as a match and police could have focused their manhunt on him. But none of those tools were available in 1937, and I kept reading, knowing that old-fashioned police and legal work would be the only tools available as the State of California tried to find out if they had the real killer.

REPORTERS WERE WITH Isabelle Dyer that day and she was giving them more confused details every time they saw her.

"I wanted to kill myself when I was washing the blood from his dungarees. I believed he was guilty even before they found the bodies, but I didn't dare tell anyone. When he came home after the murders he told me to keep my mouth shut or he'd slap me around. He told me to lie to the police and say he was home all day Saturday. I was his slave. He beat me with his heavy belt once. I was afraid to tell."

FINGER-POINTING

Inglewood, California
July 7, 1937

ON JULY 7, the *Inglewood Daily News* was full of reports of people trying to lay blame for Dyer's crime.

Someone sent a letter to the City Council criticizing Chief Campbell for how the case was handled, among other things, accusing the police of delaying the search for the missing girls and calling for a full investigation of their actions. The letter was signed by an "I. Backus" but no such person ever surfaced, and a Mrs. Backus, who, curiously, was at the City Council's evening session on July 6, denied any knowledge of the letter.

Whatever the source, Councilman Ernst Leibacher defended Campbell and the police force. He informed the council that he'd received a complete written report from the chief and every other officer who had any connection with the case. He noted that the letter writer was off by almost seven hours as to the time the missing persons report was made.

The interim mayor, Everett Simmons, also supported the force. "I went to police headquarters at 10 o'clock that night. Every available officer was searching and Captain Muir had already notified the LA Sheriff's office and officials in neighboring towns. I stayed with the department until the bodies were found and they were working around the clock."

Mrs. Harry Evans of Pasadena also wrote the City Council and blasted the swimming pool attendant who saw the girls on their way out of the park that Saturday and who heard them say they were going to hunt rabbits. Mrs. Evans demanded to know why the woman hadn't asked with whom they were going or any other details about their plans. And why had the City hired such an incompetent?

Mayor Simmons quickly informed the meeting that the City did not hire the swimming pool attendant. She was a WPA employee. Councilman Leibacher didn't miss the chance to point out on record that "the WPA is evidently not very careful who they hire."

Meanwhile, the Los Angeles newspapers reported that the WPA employee who supervised Dyer and other crossing guards was criticizing Chief Campbell because the supervisor recommended that Dyer be fired and Campbell had blocked the move. The WPA supervisor, C. H. Sanders, addressed reporters on the 7th to set things straight. He told them he never recommended to Chief Campbell or anyone else that Dyer be terminated. "So far as the records go, Dyer had one of the best records as a crossing guard of anybody in the service. No one ever officially or indirectly complained to the WPA about Dyer."

Councilman Leibacher talked with reporters after the council meeting that night and pointed them to what he identified as the real weak link in the chain. He explained there are perverts and degenerates at large and the police are powerless under present laws to do anything about it because parents are unwilling to press charges.

He told the story of a local garage employee who molested two little girls on separate occasions in the months before the triple murders. Witnesses saw him both times and reported him. The garage fired him but when police and the DA's office investigated the cases further, the parents refused to press charges because they feared the publicity.

All the accusers were apparently unmoved by an op-ed piece published just two days earlier in which the Inglewood Daily News editor seemed to anticipate the finger-pointing that would follow. He had instead urged the community to consider a different explanation for—and response to—the tragedy:

A few years ago Stanford University professors, after a long period of investigation and research, came to the conclusion that sex killers could definitely be detected. They psychoanalyzed one suspect, and all were agreed that the subject was potentially dangerous and was capable of committing a horrible crime. Less than one month later he had committed such a crime. The answer, of course, is an end of sob-sister stuff and sentimentality, and instead the use of psychoanalysis, a reasonably accurate science. Particularly should those who are designated to serve as school crossing watchmen be subjected to examination of this kind.

IT WAS INEVITABLE that a crime like this would push the collective thinking to a place where they thought they could identify and stop sex offenders before they ever start. Profiling, as we know it today, has become an invaluable tool for investigators trying to solve crimes, particularly serial murders or rapes, after the fact. But profiling as a predictive tool to deny people jobs or places to live runs afoul of our law that people are innocent until proven guilty. We must wait until someone is convicted of a crime before they can be so labeled, which is just what we do today with our sex offender registration laws—laws that have their genesis in my family's tragedy.

Shortly after the Dyer case, Dr. Paul de River—whose early analysis of Dyer is considered one of the earliest recorded forensic profiles in the United States and who would later become a controversial and mostly discredited figure because of his dubious involvement in the infamous Black Dahlia murder case—founded the first Sex Offense Bureau within the Los Angeles Police Department. His profile didn't lead police to Dyer, nor did it accurately describe Dyer on many counts: Dyer was in his thirties, not his twenties, he had no criminal record other than an arrest for burglary and some police pickups for vagrancy, and there was no evidence that Dyer manifested any tendencies for pedophilia and/or sadism. Nonetheless, de River saw then what we know today—that sex offenders, particularly those who prey on children, are unique in their psychological makeup, and those features can sometimes help identify perpetrators, both potential and actual.

To that end, Dr. de River and his assistants in the new Sex Offense Bureau examined anyone charged with a "morals offense," no matter how seemingly minor. They would identify and record tendencies and propensities, just as the *Inglewood Daily News* editor had suggested.

Paul Radin described the system in his 1951 book *12 Against Crime*:

> Under the system established by [de River], whenever a sex criminal or suspect is arrested, he is fingerprinted, photographed, placed in a line-up for observation by police and detectives, and then brought to a soundproof room where he is given psychiatric and physical examinations.
>
> Dr. de River probes thoroughly into the man's family background, his past personal history, any venereal-disease history, criminal record, and makes a searching study of his sex impulses. The psychiatric examination not only reveals whether the prisoner is medically and legally sane, but also determines his intelligence.
>
> The prisoner is typed as to any sexual perversions or peculiarities, his method of operation, his physical make-up.
>
> All this information is kept on file in the Sex Offense Bureau, together with a photograph of the prisoner. The purpose is to have on file a complete breakdown on all sex criminals so that whenever a sex crime occurs the detailed information in the bureau may provide the information leading directly to the wanted man.

Law enforcement agencies all over California—and the country for that matter—could then access the assessments to identify potential offenders when a child went missing or a rape victim reported an attack. An agency could send out an alert on the teletype or a detective would call other agencies and ask them to send a list of all their "perv perps." These assessments were the early version of the modern electronic database and much like the FBI's Violent Criminal Apprehension Program (ViCAP) today. The system was crude, but it marked the beginning of law enforcement's and society's realization that these offenders could not be deterred through traditional means and that we ought to expect the worst from known offenders because they would surely strike again.

And they did, many more times in Los Angeles in the late thirties and early forties. In 1942, armed with all the data from his work in the Sex Offense Bureau, de River published *The Sexual Criminal*, in which he analyzed four high-profile offenders, including Dyer, and in 1947, he helped author a bill introduced by California Assemblyman Don Fields. The bill ultimately became California's Penal Code Section 290, the first legislatively mandated sex offender registration program in the state and the nation, and the model for registries we have today all around the country.

Today, because of sex offender registries and what we know from studying such offenders, children are usually with their parents or some other adult keeping a watchful eye, and offenders never have the chance to get close. Most people are on the lookout, even in small towns where the threat seems remote.

But more contemporary cases—many from California, including the cases of Polly Klass, Jaycee Lee Dugard, and Danielle Van Damm, and others from across the country, like the disturbing Jerry Sandusky tragedy—remind us that the threat is often very near and doesn't always look the way we thought it would. Sometimes even when we talk to our children, as my grandmother did just the day before the murders when Eddie the Sailor tried to get Olive to go rabbit hunting, predators use their imaginative cunning to lure trusting children.

My family's tragedy seemed to be a turning point in this facet of California's legal history and a turning away from a simpler way of life, permanently altering the landscape of sunny, carefree days in places like Centinela Park.

ON JULY 7, while the defense psychiatrists were examining Dyer and with his wife in protective custody, police investigators told reporters they'd searched the Dyers' home and found the knife Dyer allegedly used to cut the pieces of rope he used to strangle the girls. He'd described the knife in his testimony before the grand jury and investigators claimed they found it right where Dyer said it would be—hidden in a box of jumbled personal effects. Also reportedly found in his shack house, several pieces of rope that investigators hoped the crime lab would be able to confirm was just like the rope found around the girls' necks.

Under further questioning on July 8, Isabelle Dyer elaborated on what she'd told reporters the day before, that when Albert came home Saturday night his clothes were filled with burrs and hay and that he demanded she wash his blue jeans immediately. Then he threatened her that if police asked her about him, she better tell him that he'd been home all day Saturday.

And so, the world waited for Albert Dyer to plead guilty. He appeared for his arraignment on July 8, but his newly appointed public defender, Frederic Vercoe, asked the judge for more time. Among other things, Vercoe wanted to have more doctors examine Dyer to determine whether an insanity defense was still a possibility.

Vercoe's diligence on that front was understandable. He still couldn't believe some of the things his client said to him. Dyer had said to Vercoe just that morning, "I'd be willing to report every month to a probation officer. I'd like to join the Navy. I'll bet that would make a man of me."

The judge granted Vercoe extra time to prepare his case and the world would have to wait another week for Dyer's plea, but the press was already sending the accused killer to death row. The *Inglewood Daily News* headlines on July 9 announced that Dyer was expected to plead guilty on Monday: "Will Be Taken to Death Row, San Quentin, by Next Friday," "Can Be Sentenced To Hang Even Though He Pleads Guilty, Says Fitts."

The people of Inglewood breathed a collective sigh of relief. Justice would be swift and certain.

THE ARRAIGNMENT

Hall of Justice, Los Angeles, California
July 12, 1937

"JUDGE, YOUR HONOR, I plead not guilty!" Dyer shouted in response to the charge of first-degree murder for the death of Madeline Everett.

The officers in the special courtroom detail guarding Dyer tensed and braced for a possible rush on the defendant, but the spectators packing the courtroom were too shocked to move. They could only gasp.

The judge read the second charge—exactly like the first except for the death of Melba Marie Everett. "Judge, Your Honor, I plead not guilty!" Dyer again shouted. And again, the same plea for the death of Jeanette Marjorie Stephens.

District Attorney Fitts was not amused and informed the judge that the state was ready to proceed as soon as possible, asking the court set the earliest possible date for trial.

Public Defender Vercoe again pleaded for more time, noting how the prosecution had already been investigating and preparing the case for several weeks.

Judge Ambrose gave Vercoe just four weeks, setting the matter for trial on August 6. Vercoe started packing up his briefcase and the bailiffs began moving toward Dyer, but Judge Ambrose wasn't finished. He put Vercoe on notice that he would not entertain any motions for a substitution of attorneys in the case.

"Since Dyer has no funds, there could be only one motive that would cause private counsel to take the case. That would be publicity-seeking, which this court will not tolerate."

Vercoe and his team would be on the case for the duration.

The bailiffs escorted Albert Dyer out of the courtroom and back to the changing room, where he surrendered the white shirt and slacks Vercoe had brought for him. He got back into his pajama-like jail denims and shuffled along to his cell.

WITHIN HOURS, THE DA's office announced that fifteen-year-old Dorothy Reitz signed a statement in which she recounted seeing Albert Dyer on three separate occasions on that Saturday morning in Centinela Park. She detailed how he was holding a little girl's hand by the swimming pool. Dorothy described the girl as looking just like Jeanette Stephens.

BACK AT HIS office, Vercoe must have felt the shot across his bow, but he had work to do. Four weeks to prepare wasn't enough time in any trial, but it was a dangerously short window in this one, where he couldn't count on anything, especially his client. And he was already feeling the pressures of defending someone who had confessed, but he turned that into an opportunity to publicly explain his duty and obligations to the cause of justice.

He issued a statement that newspapers, including the *Los Angeles Times*, ran the next day:

> *They (the authorities) obtained a confession of guilt from the defendant. Wide publicity has been given to this case and the evidence is in the possession of the District Attorney. Nevertheless, there are persistent rumors that the wrong man has been arrested and charged with the crimes and a considerable number of persons, more or less familiar with the facts of the case, have expressed a doubt which exists in their minds as to whether Albert Dyer is the man who committed the ghastly and horrible crimes. Under these circumstances, there should be a full and fair hearing at a trial of all the available and material evidence relevant to the charge.*

The *Inglewood Daily News* did not agree with Vercoe. The editor accused everyone involved of agreeing to go to trial so the parties could parade evidence, "not to convince the court and jury of the defendant's guilt, but to satisfy the people that the right man is in custody."

> *The startling plea of "not guilty" entered yesterday by Albert Dyer of Inglewood to the triple slaying of three local girls may be entitled 'skirmishing' but it offers a strange commentary on a people who have been called the most emotional in the world. Many of the people who were demanding that the slayer be captured in the days immediately following the discovery of the crime, are now insisting that the wrong man has been taken. This is Americania—1937 edition.*

The trial would be nothing but "another opportunity for publicity seekers to bask in the calcium spotlight." He accused the major metro newspapers of building up "out of the figments of their imagination, a straw man with a moustache, an 'Eddie the Sailor' hombre of fiction in a battered car, who failed to materialize."

> *If, from the beginning, solution of the case had been approached on a basis of scientific criminology, and not on publicity, it would not have been necessary yesterday to have delayed the sentence of the man in custody. For Albert Dyer is the only man under the canopy of heaven, except the autopsy surgeon, who knew how the three little girls had been violated, and his confession on the day of his capture and repeated thereafter, included that information.*

THE TEMPTATION IS understandable. When the suspect knows certain details that only the killer could have known, why not dispense with the rule of law and march them to the gallows? The temptation must have been unbelievably strong in this case.

So why did Vercoe take Dyer to trial? It's an important question, and most lawyers field this type of question at dinner parties more than any other. "How can someone defend a guilty man? He confessed!"

And like every other lawyer, I explain that a defense attorney's role is not to decide guilt or innocence but to protect a defendant's constitutional rights—to be sure the prosecution proves its case beyond a reasonable doubt. When a defendant has confessed, it may seem unnecessary to force the state to meet this burden, but a defense attorney's role is to put the state to that test so we can be certain that justice is served—legally.

Nonetheless, defense attorneys don't go to trial very often. About 95 percent of criminal cases are plea-bargained precisely because the defense has determined that the state has a tight, legal case and trial is futile or risky. So, when a defendant pleads not guilty and goes to trial, we can safely assume their attorney has found holes in the state's case or, as we see in cases of wrongful convictions, they've found indicators of police or prosecutorial misconduct—and the only way to find the truth is to take that day in court and hope that a jury sees what you see.

Of course, sometimes defense attorneys go to trial because they have reason to believe their client is actually innocent, which must have been the case with Albert Dyer, because his attorneys had every reason not to go to trial.

No defense attorney wants that case—nobody wants to be the person who defended the sadistic pedophile who murdered three little girls, delaying justice and closure for the grief-stricken families and the community. It would have been so much easier to say, *Look, Albert, you are going to hang. If you plead guilty, maybe we can get the prosecution to agree to life in prison.* Dyer was so afraid of the noose, he would surely have said yes to that offer.

And contrary to popular misconceptions, a public defender is not going to make extra money from the case, either. They do not earn fees based on the complexity of the case or the notoriety of their client. They are paid a government salary and then, no matter what the verdict, they head back to the office and begin working on behalf of another criminal defendant who cannot afford a private attorney.

Further, public defenders know they'll be working at a marked disadvantaged in financial and investigatory resources. In most jurisdictions, public defenders' offices are woefully underfunded compared to well-supported police and prosecutors, so most criminal cases start out with a deck stacked in favor of the prosecution. Deputy public defender Ellery Cuff, who was part of Vercoe's trial team, described to the press the exact same problem during Dyer's case:

> There are no funds available in the public defender's office for a thorough investigation. The four investigators who have been working for us have been volunteers serving without pay.

Deputy public defender William Neely:

> There are a dozen items of extreme importance to us in this case, which we have been unable to explain satisfactorily. There are no means at our command to run these matters to earth.

And Vercoe on the added challenges with a defendant like Dyer:

> I have had nearly 25 years' experience in the handling of criminal cases but the Dyer case is one of the most difficult I have ever handled. The sub-normal mental condition of the defendant, he being rated mentally as ten years of age or less, [makes] it difficult to reach a satisfying conclusion as to the case.

So, despite all these reasons not to go trial, they did, but perhaps that was a bad decision? Another cause of wrongful convictions is the ineffective assistance of counsel—bad lawyering—and I was understandably curious early on about Dyer's team. Were they inexperienced? Had they fumbled cases in the past? Anything negative to suggest they made missteps in assessing the evidence?

On the contrary, these men were some of the best, and they were part of legal history. Los Angeles County established the first public defender office in the nation in 1914, nearly fifty years before the landmark ruling in *Gideon v. Wainwright* (1963), in which the US Supreme Court required government-appointed counsel for any indigent defendants facing felony charges, giving official birth to the public defender concept. The Los Angeles office was way ahead of its time, and the staff and procedures there were considered cutting edge for that era. Frederic Vercoe was part of that history, having served as the chief public defender for nearly ten years when his office was appointed to represent Dyer.

Deputy Ellery Cuff graduated from the prestigious USC School of Law and he, too, had been with the public defender's office for nearly ten years when he took on the Dyer case. He went on to head the office just eleven years later.

William Neely was similarly distinguished. Nine years after the Dyer case, the Los Angeles Board of Supervisors tapped Neely to head the office, and then three years later, California governor—and later US Supreme Court Justice—Earl Warren appointed Neely to the California Superior Court bench, where he served as a judge in the psychiatric and criminal department. Following an interest that may have been sparked or further solidified during the Dyer case, he was also credited with organizing the Mental Health Foundation, later to become the Los Angeles County Mental Health Association, and he lectured often on forensic medicine at the USC Medical School.

No, these were talented lawyers. The only conclusion is that Vercoe and his team saw enough holes in the evidence, enough real questions about Dyer's innocence, to justify the impossibly tough road of forcing the state to prove its case to a jury.

ACROSS THE COUNTRY, readers were stunned by a real-life horror story in the July 12 edition of *Time* magazine. It was entitled "Three Little Girls," but it was all about a child killer who posed as a school crossing guard.

HASKELL WRIGHT

Hall of Justice, Los Angeles, California
July 13, 1937

WHILE DYER'S DEFENSE attorneys began organizing their legal fight for Dyer's life, Haskell Wright continued to lead the public charge that Dyer was not the killer. The *Inglewood Daily News* headlined Wright's efforts, reporting "Local Man In Move to Prove Dyer Innocent." He submitted an affidavit to the district attorney's office and enlisted others to do the same. And on July 13, the grand jury assembled again to hear testimony.

But Wright's claims went nowhere. He testified that Dyer was not the man he'd seen with the children in the park on Friday before the murders. He claimed Dyer was a pathological liar and couldn't be believed.

Bill Simpson from the DA's office easily disposed of Wright. "There is no contention upon the part of the State, nor by Dyer himself, that he was in the park the day before the abductions."

And worse yet, one of Wright's group, Charles Atkins, revealed on the witness stand that he never actually swore to the affidavit that was submitted in his name, and that when he read it in court, he realized it was only partially correct. Someone—Wright?—wrote in the affidavit that Atkins saw Mr. and Mrs. Dyer in front of Atkins's Commercial Street shop at 5 p.m. on Saturday. Atkins said he never saw Mrs. Dyer and that he saw only Mr. Dyer but he couldn't be sure what time it was.

If all that wasn't enough, the next day, Dyer confessed again.

Prosecutors Simpson and Williams met with Dyer and Vercoe. "Let's go over it again," Simpson said, "just to be sure."

"I didn't do it."

"Then why did you say you did?" Simpson asked.

"I was scared and didn't know what was happening. I was out of my mind," Dyer replied.

"Are you in your right mind now?"

"Yes, I'm all right now, that's why I want you to know I didn't do it."

Gene Williams leaned forward and took another approach.

"As a matter of fact, you changed your mind after you learned you were going to hang, didn't you?"

And without hesitating, Dyer responded, "Yes, I did."

Williams switched Dyer's train of thought just like that. "All right then now, tell us the truth—by the way there's some confusion as to which way you took those children into the hills. Now how was it?"

And Dyer began confessing again. "This time I am going to tell the truth," he said.

THAT SAME DAY, Police Chief Oscar Campbell announced the end of the WPA school crossing guard program. Funds for the program were exhausted, and maybe the city would bring back some guards in the fall when school started again, but for now there would be no more guards. He added sternly that any future guards would be subjected to a rigid inspection of their records and backgrounds. The reporters didn't ask any further questions. Everyone knew there would never again be school crossing guards in Inglewood.

CASUALTIES

**Office of the District Attorney, Los Angeles, California
July 13, 1937**

THE OFFICIAL RECORD reveals that my grandparents lost two daughters in 1937. But digging deeper, it seems they may have lost—at least partly—another one. My Aunt Olive became part of a strange side story in the press, but she was arguably another casualty of that dark summer.

While Haskell Wright testified before the grand jury, Olive was still in protective custody over at the DA's office. Bess Bailey, a deputy sheriff who was sitting with her, reported that out of the blue Olive volunteered that Mr. Wright had molested her in the park during the previous year.

Deputy Bailey alerted officials with the DA's office and after Wright finished testifying in Dyer's defense, the DA's office took him into "technical custody" so they could look into Olive's shocking claims. Wright was stunned. Everyone was. The timing of Olive's revelation was curious enough, but the accusation was wholly unexpected.

Later, the DA's office arranged to have Wright meet his accuser so they could all get to the bottom of this. They met on neutral ground at the sheriff's office. Wright brought his attorney, DA Fitts brought two other deputy district attorneys to observe, and, of course, there was Olive. She was eleven years old. Wright immediately confronted her.

"Young lady, you are not telling the truth!"

Olive held fast to her claim and again explained that Wright molested her in the park.

Wright denied her claims. Olive stuck to her story.

DA Fitts later explained to reporters that "the matter is so grave that I have no alternative but to present the facts to the Grand Jury. We are not prejudging this matter. Two people are telling exactly the opposite stories. With the help of an unbiased grand jury we may eventually get the truth."

Wright's attorney countered and told reporters, "The girl's entire story is ridiculous."

Wright was released to his attorney's custody and the matter was set for further grand jury testimony on July 15.

OLIVE TESTIFIED FOR two hours on the 15th, claiming that at least four men attacked her in the park at various times. She clarified that Wright only molested her, not attacked her. She spoke so softly that the judge asked her several times to speak up. She raised her head a little and tried to be louder, but she always ended up looking at her lap and almost whispering her testimony.

In sharp contrast, Wright came armed with his attorney and ten very vocal character witnesses. He vehemently denied any wrong-doing, staring at Olive and accusing her again and again of lying. One of his supporters even suggested that Olive was accusing him in retaliation for Wright carrying out his duties at the park.

"Those children practically lived in Centinela Park. On a dozen occasions Wright has had to chase them home. This is undoubtedly the result," proclaimed R. B. Hawthorne, who operated the park popcorn stand.

Mrs. Craycroft, the pool matron who knew all the Everett girls so well, also supported Wright, testifying that Olive's story was "a figment of her imagination."

Five boys ranging from nine to eleven years old also testified that they'd never seen Wright around any girls in the park.

No girls were called to testify.

Officials from the DA's office told the *Los Angeles Times* that while Olive had been in protective custody at their office, she steadily added to the list of names of men who allegedly molested her. One official said the strain of the preceding weeks "may have affected the imagination of the Everett child."

The wire service dispatched a photo later that day of Olive after she testified, sitting in the lobby area outside the grand jury room. She has on a beautiful light dress and white shoes, and a ribbon headband holding back her curled hair. And for some reason, she's smiling brightly.

The matter was set for continued grand jury testimony on July 21. The DA's office continued to hold Olive in protective custody.

I FOUND NO other reference to the July 21 hearing or any further action on my aunt's claims.

A friend of the family told me—some seventy years later—"Olive wouldn't make something up, she wouldn't lie. Who was it, who did she accuse?" The reaction suggested that the friend already knew the claims were true and wanted to confirm it was the same person she knew to have done such a thing. It sure struck me that way. But when I told the friend about Wright, she seemed surprised, or at the very least, genuinely unsure of who he was.

I've also often wondered why Olive would testify before a grand jury about that sort of thing when most kids can't even tell their own parents. And if she had told her parents, surely they would have notified police or shored up her accusations with their own testimony, but there are no reports of their reaction or involvement.

It's difficult to understand and especially hard to sort out because Olive was in protective custody with the DA's office beginning almost immediately after the girls went missing because she had so much eyewitness information about the Friday afternoon in the park when Eddie the Sailor approached her and her sisters, so reports on her are scarce. But because of what may have been legitimate claims of molestation, and because she was at the center of such troubling and public events so soon after losing her sisters, she may have carried a double burden when time marched on after the events of 1937.

My Aunt Olive was one of those people who lived behind a wall. When you approached her, it was tangible, and behind it you knew there was a great heaviness. You could feel it—and see it. She was extremely overweight, and that weight was like a fortress around her. Friends told me that she started gaining weight just after the murders, eating to ease her pain. Maybe she unconsciously amassed that weight to protect herself. After what she endured in 1937 and perhaps in the year or so before that if her molestation claims were true, I can understand why she might feel the need to fortify her defenses.

Despite all of it, she devoted her life to helping others. She was a registered nurse, which makes so much sense now. Even in the newspaper photographs of her right after the girls disappeared, while the family was tortured with waiting for news, she seemed to be comforting my grandparents and little Carl, which is extraordinary for an eleven-year-old girl who's worrying about two beloved sisters. But that was Olive, and a family doctor always said she was the absolute best nurse in the hospital.

Early in my research, around 2010, I reached out to my half-sister Madlynne to ask if she knew anything about the girls. We were never in very close touch but I always loved hearing from her or seeing her at the occasional family gathering. I wondered if she felt our family history slipping away after our dad died in 1987, and our Uncle Carl in 2004. She did. I wondered if she'd ever heard about the girls. She had.

Like me, when she was younger, she'd heard only that something terrible had happened. She also learned that my dad and his first wife named her—Madlynne Marie—after the girls, so she was especially curious about the story. She thought our aunt Olive would know the most, having been so close to the girls but old enough at the time to remember. So, in 2000, she wrote to Olive, knowing Olive had always been somewhat reclusive and knowing she might not hear anything back. But eventually, Olive responded and her reply is such a gift, with stories about our dad, our grandparents and even our great-grandparents. Most importantly, it's a treasure of the few things we know about Marie and Madeline, gleaned from somewhere other than records of their tragic deaths. Her observations are especially precious because I could feel even in a letter how difficult it was for her to go back there. "Then June 26th came." I could almost hear her finishing the thought, *and everything changed.*

She wrote "I think of my sisters and wonder how they would look, what their ambitions would have been. But I won't know any of that until I join them, as I know I will." She was also keenly aware that she probably narrowly escaped death herself because she might have been with the girls on that fateful day. "As young as I was, I knew that my life had been spared for a reason."

I had wanted so badly to talk with Olive about our family's story, about her experience and about Marie and Madeline, but Olive died thirteen days after she wrote to my sister, years before I started researching the case. Her letter is all I have.

I HAVE VERY few details about the rest of my family during that time, but at least I have some, and many of which came to me rather fortuitously, so I'm especially grateful.

Because I stayed with my dad in Reno after my parents divorced, I finished high school and college there. My dad died there. Eventually, I went on to law school in San Diego but I would go back to Reno often to visit friends and my dad's grave, as I did on the fifth anniversary of his death in 1992. He was buried in a beautiful spot in the forest near Lake Tahoe, and it was an idyllic setting to sit and remember. But on this particular day, I stayed longer than I usually did and I felt a deep, but unexplained connection, like he was there.

When I arrived back home in San Diego, my phone was ringing as I walked in from the airport—"Hello, are you Pamela Everett, Perley Everett's daughter?"

"Yes, I am."

"Well, I'm June Quimby and I grew up with your dad. I was just going through some things today and I found some photographs of him I thought you might like. It took quite a lot for me to track you down," she laughed.

I remembered my graveside experience, and told this voice from out of the blue that she would never believe where I'd just been visiting. We talked for some time and she encouraged me to visit her at her home north of Los Angeles any time.

And some months later, over tea in her living room, she told me about my dad. He was best friends with her big brother Cal Hazley. She talked about how handsome he was, how his smile was like none she'd ever seen, and how sad everyone was when he went off to the Navy after high school. She confessed that she was probably a little bit in love with him. Then she brought out his portrait from Navy boot camp in 1942. It was priceless.

I asked about the rest of my family—where did they live, how did they live, did she know my Aunt Olive and Uncle Carl? She did. And she gave me all those descriptive terms for my grandparents like "Bostonian" and "proper" and "very New England."

"And then when your dad came to live with us, I didn't see as much of your grandparents."

"Why did he live with you?"

"Well, you know—or maybe you don't—it was after the girls."

I told her that I knew just a little but that nobody ever talked about it. I asked her to tell me about my aunts, but every time she tried, she'd have to check her emotions and she finally said it was too difficult to talk about. She said they were wonderful little girls. "It was a tragedy." And that was all.

Still, she was able to tell me more about why my dad lived with her family. She said during much of the ordeal, my grandmother would often seem to be waiting expectantly on the living room couch, right around the time the girls would have been getting out of school, even though it was summertime. My dad would try to get her interested in something else, my grandfather, too. We needn't wait and watch, they would tell her.

But the worst part was the dining table. They didn't eat as much during that turbulent time, everyone was so unsettled, but when she could, my grandmother was trying to give the family some sense of routine, some comforts of the normal life they'd led before June 26. So, she'd prepare food and set the table.

With two places set for the girls. Right where they always sat. Plates, silverware, and napkins arranged with care. As if, any minute, they might come down the hall and round the corner into the dining room.

June said my dad came to her family's house one afternoon with a few things packed in a bag. He didn't say anything but they all knew he needed a sanctuary. They welcomed him with loving gestures of home without talking about any of it. When my dad saw Mrs. Hazley that evening getting dinner ready in the kitchen, he thanked her for having him.

"Oh Perley, stop that. You're part of our family. We'll just put another bean in the pot!"

My dad never lived at the Everett house on Hazel Street again.

BY ALL ACCOUNTS, including June Hazley's, my grandmother's hair turned gray almost overnight beginning right after the girls went missing. Olive wrote in her letter in 2000, "When I saw my mom again [after being in protective custody], her hair was not the dark brown as I remembered but snow white." Her beautiful white hair was like her signature in those later years when I knew her, but I'd never known how long it had been that way or how it must have reminded everyone about the day their lives changed forever.

Most people probably assumed that my grandmother must have gone a little crazy during that time, but I'm not so sure. Her intelligence and poise were matched only by her deep religious faith. I suspect she turned the matter over to some higher power and perhaps she hoped and prayed that indeed miracles happen and God would return her girls, safe and sound. She would always say, "God works in mysterious ways." My sister Madlynne recalled a Bible lesson that one should always set an extra place at the table. Madlynne could imagine, and I can too, my grandma taking that teaching to heart, setting places for the girls, and hoping her God would bring them home.

ABOUT ELEVEN YEARS after my dad died, around 1998, I visited my Uncle Carl at his home in Bellflower, California, and I asked him about the murders. It was like all the air went out of the room and he was visibly shaken by the mere mention of something from that period. All he could say for a while was "it was an interesting time . . . very interesting." I probed, but carefully.

Finally, his wife coaxed him along. She brought out a faded and torn copy of *American Detective* magazine from October 1937, with the cover story entitled "The Smiling Monster of Inglewood." It was the first evidence I'd seen that the tragedy really happened. I was amazed. The article was long and detailed with photos of the girls' bodies, the little shoes, and my grandmother and Olive. I wanted to absorb every bit of it right then but I wanted to talk with my uncle—I could read later.

But he couldn't talk about it. He kept saying only that it was an "interesting time." He was visibly nervous, almost childlike in his discomfort. I tried to remind myself that he was so young when it happened, only five, so he probably remembered only that his sisters were gone and everyone was acting strangely. The only thing he could say with any certainty was that my dad left after the girls were killed. "He went to live somewhere else." And he remembered that his mother never seemed the same. He too mentioned how her hair went white overnight.

Then unexpectedly, he got up, went and opened two beers, and brought out a picture to the kitchen table. It was a photo of him and the girls just a week or so before they died. Marie is in the middle with little Madeline on her right and my Uncle Carl on her left. Their arms are all entwined, the summer sun brightening their beaming faces. He set it on the table and we both studied it. It was the first picture I'd seen of the girls and I thought, they really did exist, he really knew them, and he lived through losing them. I looked up to check his reaction and he said softly, "We were inseparable." I smiled.

And then he added, "Still are."

AROUND THE SAME time my dad moved in with the Hazleys, my dad's little brother, ten-year-old Merle—"Junior"—ran away from his grandfather's home in Los Angeles where he'd been staying since the girls disappeared. He'd run away several times before, so nobody was very surprised. In fact, Cal Hazley's dad always talked to Junior about it because he'd run away when he was a kid too, but Junior kept leaving whenever it suited him. Everyone was sure Junior would turn up. And he did. But none of the newspapers that covered the Dyer story ever mentioned him and there are no photographs of him from that time. He would remain a mystery to me as he had most of my life.

I don't believe I ever met him, but my sisters and I all remember my dad making vague, mostly negative, references to him when we were growing up. He allegedly rode the rails a lot and was mixed up in a less than law-abiding life. Somebody, maybe my dad, called him the black sheep and that's how I remember him even though I never saw him and I never knew him as my uncle. I always picture him, even today, as a stranger with dark hair and dark clothing.

So, I was surprised when I found a photograph of him from 1938 in my grandmother's scrapbook and saw that he looked almost exactly like my dad—smiling, expressive, and seemingly warm, no black hair or dark clothes. And in one shot, he has an obviously caring arm around my grandfather.

Still, something happened on his road to adulthood and I'll never know if he was truly a bad apple or just another casualty of the events in 1937. He died in the late '90s in Southern California, but other than that I couldn't find any records of him.

Whatever the case, he too is part of my family and knowing that he endured losing the girls has brought him into my heart. After I looked at his photographs for a while, I whispered something I'd never said before, "Uncle Junior."

NO MATTER WHAT anguish they were going through at home and in their hearts, my grandparents were composed in making a public statement of thanks, which newspapers ran on July 15:

We desire to extend our heartfelt thanks to the hundreds of persons in Southern California and throughout the nation who have, by sympathetic act and deed, helped us to bear our tragic loss. Although it is to be devoutly hoped that no parents will ever again have to suffer the loss of children in the same way as we did, the one bright spot in the whole sordid affair is the outpouring of sympathy by friends and strangers alike. It is gratifying to learn that in times of deepest sorrow, there are hundreds to give life to that old adage, 'a touch of sorrow makes the whole world kin.' We are grateful also to those who contributed to the fund raised through the medium of the Daily News, and although this can never replace our departed loved ones, it will, in a measure, assist in re-establishing us as productive units of the community. May God bless all those who had a part in this undertaking.

THE SHOWUP

Hall of Justice, Los Angeles, California
July 14, 1937

THE WALLS WERE already closing in on Albert Dyer—all those confessions and recantations, the bizarre behavior at the arraignment, and the collective sigh of relief police and the community were breathing because someone—anyone—was in custody. And then the police conducted a showup, and you could almost hear the nails being pounded into the coffin.

The showup is a highly suggestive procedure where police show eyewitnesses a single suspect. By its very design, the showup tells witnesses there is only one suspect and here he is. Unlike traditional lineups, where the suspect is grouped with fillers, a witness to a showup has no alternatives to choose other than the single suspect before them and so, not surprisingly, they are predisposed to say *yes, that's the man.*

A showup becomes even more dangerous when it's conducted too long after the crime—even hours or a day—because memories fade so quickly and witnesses may already have been tainted with media reports about the suspected perpetrator and other facts. Worse yet, police desperate to find a suspect to preserve public safety after a crime have conducted showups with the suspect in the back of a squad car, or, in one amazing case, with the suspect wearing a pantyhose stocking over his head because the perpetrator reportedly wore one during the crime.

And these practices were apparently in full swing during the Dyer investigation. F. C. North, the park's recreation director, explained months later in a sworn affidavit that detectives "were always having us go in to look at any kind of a suspect. We usually had a sort of a sales talk before we looked at a man, giving us his record, and they would say he was a degenerate or a son of a so and so who has got a record and he ought to hang, and they would take us in to look at the man. If we didn't recognize him, they would ask us why and what is wrong with him."

The practice became so problematic that the US Supreme Court, thirty years after Dyer's case, condemned it as "so unnecessarily suggestive and conducive to irreparable mistaken identification" that it violates a defendant's constitutional rights.

But that ruling would not help Albert Dyer when, nearly three weeks later, police paraded him in front of a group of children who claimed to be at the park the morning the girls disappeared. They also presented him to George Reilly, the man in the Overhill office, and to Joseph Field, the WPA chauffeur who had claimed to see a man coming from the Baldwin Hills late that Saturday. Dyer came in bareheaded first and then wearing a WPA crossing guard cap. The children identified him as the man they'd seen on Saturday, June 26. Reilly said Dyer "resembled" the man he saw on Overhill Drive that day. Field said Dyer looked "similar" to the man he saw coming from the Baldwin Hills late Saturday afternoon.

A chilling photograph from that day shows Dyer in front of a height chart, flanked by an officer and investigator, grinning and looking somewhat amused and confused in denims and his crossing guard cap. Dyer's defense attorneys would argue at trial that none of the other men presented separately at the showup looked anything like Albert Dyer, but to no avail.

A traditional lineup, where the suspect is presented with non-suspect "fillers," wouldn't have helped him either because, as in the Ronald Cotton case and so many others, witnesses assume the perpetrator is in the lineup, so they tend to compare and pick someone who is the closest likeness to the person they think they saw, even when the suspect is not even present.

Today, social scientists tell us that a much more reliable lineup method is the sequential double-blind photo array, where a neutral administrator or a computer presents the suspects, eliminating detectives and others who can inadvertently support certain identifications with bodily or verbal cues. Research reveals that when people see suspects in this format, they are more likely to pick the actual perpetrator rather than picking someone who looks closest to the person they think they saw. Other safeguards include videotaping lineup procedures, ensuring that fillers look as much like the eyewitness' description of the perpetrator as possible, instructing witnesses that the suspect may or may not be present in the lineup, and obtaining statements from witnesses about how confident they are about the person they've chosen.

All of these reforms can significantly reduce the risk of wrongful convictions. All too late, though, in the case of Albert Dyer.

THE DAY AFTER the showup, jail officials reported that Dyer was alternating between states of extreme calm and complete hysterics, always clutching a Bible he was barely able to read. He remained on twenty-four-hour suicide watch with two guards posted at all times.

Several days later, the *Los Angeles Times* and other papers ran a story announcing the "final link in the chain of physical evidence by which the state expects to corroborate Albert Dyer's confession." According to the reports, the small candy bag found beneath Marie's body in the ravine would be used to "clinch" the state's case against Dyer. Testing showed the bag—the type normally used for drug sundries—had contained candy, and an Inglewood drugstore confirmed that they'd run out of their usual candy bags and, on the Friday before the murders and that Saturday morning, they'd used the drug sundry bags instead.

Investigators believed the killer used the bag of candy to lure the girls to the hills and they planned to show that Dyer was the man who bought the candy. They met with the candy counter clerk who was on duty those two days and would use her to identify Dyer. Reports indicated that witnesses would testify they saw Dyer with the girls on the route to the Baldwin Hills and that he had a bag of candy in his shirt pocket.

But no matter how many times investigators worked on him, Dyer repeatedly denied buying the bag of candy.

The legal team at Vercoe's office finally responded to the reports of the "clinched" case by pleading with the public for information. They held a press conference at the *Inglewood Daily News* offices and announced that Vercoe himself was inviting anyone who had information on the case to meet with him in his office at the Hall of Justice or to leave their name with the *Inglewood Daily News* staff and a deputy public defender would contact them.

"I am anxious that the suspect have the benefit of any information which bears on the case and I am especially anxious that when the case is finally determined there will be a lifting of the pall of gloom, doom and disbelief that seems to be prevalent."

THE EXPERIMENT

Inglewood, California
July 29, 1937

DISTRICT ATTORNEY FITTS had two key witnesses who would testify they saw the three girls walking toward the Baldwin Hills on June 26. They would testify that someone was walking just ahead of the girls, and one of the witnesses, Mr. Reilly, would testify that it was a man who looked like Albert Dyer. These two witnesses were the only evidence of what happened between the time the girls left the park and the time the Boy Scouts found their bodies on June 28. This piece of the puzzle would have to be rock solid.

And it seemed to be. The district attorney's men interviewed the witnesses repeatedly and their stories hadn't changed. They were prepared to testify. Even the Japanese store owner, Kaneo Mitzutani, who knew the girls, which made her testimony so persuasive, gave perfect answers through the translator who would serve during the trial.

They were ready.

Yet, Fitts must have felt something gnawing at him, something missing. He had to make sure the jury believed the girls walked to the Baldwin Hills. If they didn't—and the defense would surely try to get them to disbelieve it—then they would never buy his witnesses' stories about how they passed by Centinela Avenue and Hazel Street, and then Overhill Drive, up toward Slauson. He had to make that walk possible.

Fitts assigned the task to his investigator Everett Davis, and on July 29, Davis and Lieutenant Sanderson from the LAPD started on foot from the corner of Centinela Avenue and Warren Lane, just

Othel Strong's mugshot, left, published in multiple newspapers July 1, 1937. (Perry Fowler, *Herald-Examiner* Collection, Los Angeles Public Library). Fred Godsey mugshot, right, published in the *LA Times* July 3, 1937. (Copyright 1937, *Los Angeles Times*. Reprinted with permission).

Albert Dyer Murder Trial, Los Angeles Hall of Justice, August 1937. (*Los Angeles Daily News* Negatives (Collection 1387). Library Special Collections, Charles E. Young Research Library, UCLA.)

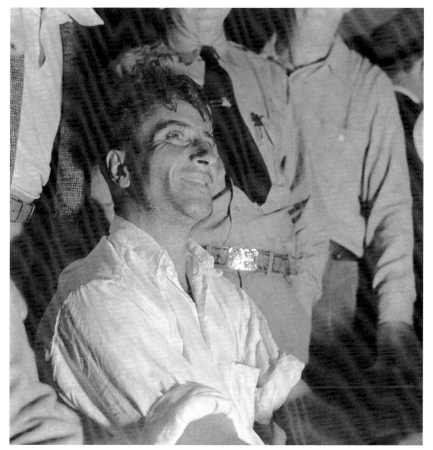

Albert Dyer After Confessing, Los Angeles Hall of Justice, July 5, 1937. (*Los Angeles Daily News* Negatives (Collection 1387). Library Special Collections, Charles E. Young Research Library, UCLA.)

Madeline Everett, Nantasket Beach, Massachusetts, 1935. (Courtesy of the author).

Melba Marie Everett, Inglewood, California 1936. (Courtesy of the author).

Deputy Los Angeles County Sheriff F. P. Dickerson exhibiting a noose and the little shoes at the Albert Dyer murder trial, August 16, 1937. (Bettman Archive/Getty Images).

Jeanette Stephens' family, June 30, 1937. (*Herald-Examiner* Collection/Los Angeles Public Library)

Olive and Carl Everett at the Everett home awaiting news of the missing girls, June 28, 1937. (*Herald-Examiner* Collection/Los Angeles Public Library).

Olive, Carl and Merle Everett at home awaiting news of the missing girls, June 28, 1937. (*Herald-Examiner* Collection/Los Angeles Public Library).

The shoes worn by murder victims Melba Marie Everett, Madeline Everett, and Jeanette Stephens, June 30, 1937. (*Herald-Examiner* Collection/Los Angeles Public Library).

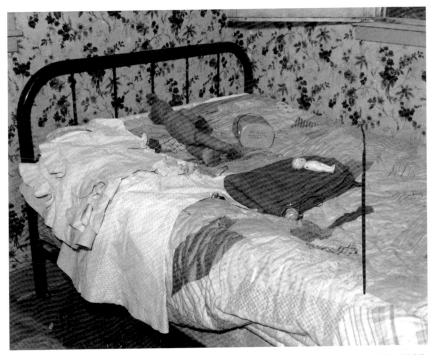

Marie and Madeline Everett's toys and blanket left in the park, June 30, 1937. (*Herald-Examiner* Collection/Los Angeles Public Library).

Inglewood Police Chief Oscar Campbell with Boy Scouts Winslow Smith, Bob Brown, and Frank Portune after the boys reported finding the girls' bodies, June 28, 1937. (Howard Ballew, *Herald-Examiner* Collection/Los Angeles Public Library).

Marie and Madeline Everett's caskets outside the Pierce Brothers Mortuary in Los Angeles, July 2, 1937. (*Herald-Examiner* Collection/Los Angeles Public Library).

Questioning of suspect Luther Dow at the Los Angeles District Attorney's Office, June 30, 1937. Left side of table: Deputy District Attorney Tom Covett and Deputy District Attorney Eugene Williams. Right side of table: Marvin Hardige and Luther Dow. (*Herald-Examiner* Collection/Los Angeles Public Library).

Albert Dyer at the police showup, Los Angeles County Hall of Justice, July 14, 1937. (*Herald-Examiner* Collection/Los Angeles Public Library).

Spectators wait outside the courtroom before the first day of Albert Dyer's trial, August 6, 1937. (*Herald-Examiner* Collection/Los Angeles Public Library).

Albert Dyer in the Los Angeles County Jail after confessing, July 5, 1937. (*Herald-Examiner* Collection/Los Angeles Public Library).

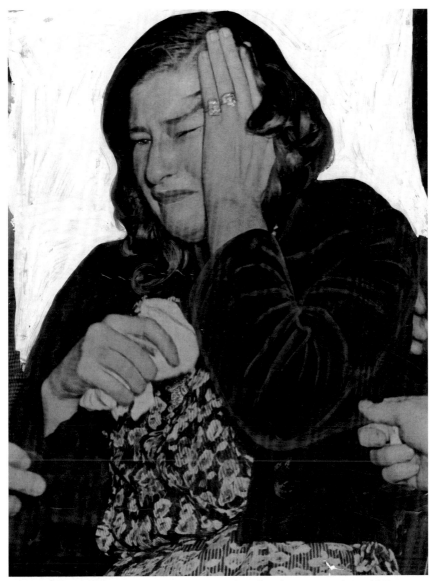

Isabelle Dyer reacting after Albert Dyer confessed, July 5, 1937. (*Herald-Examiner* Collection/Los Angeles Public Library).

Albert Dyer posing for newspaper photographers during the trial, August 1937. (*Herald-Examiner* Collection/Los Angeles Public Library).

outside the park. They watched as three little girls, aged seven, nine, and ten, set out walking ahead of them. It was 1:30 in the afternoon, just about the time Dyer and the girls would have started on their fateful walk a month earlier.

They took Centinela to Market Street, then over to Forrest, to Fairview and up Overhill Drive to Slauson, and then west on Slauson to the intersection with LaBrea. They left the road there and walked on the trail next to the bean field and over the hill to the head of the ravine. It took an hour.

Davis went down into the ravine to where the bodies were found and then back up to where he left Sanderson and the girls. Seventeen more minutes.

Then the convoy headed back out to the road, to a waiting police car. They piled happily into the backseat, looking wide-eyed in wonder at the policemen and their equipment. The girls were fine—no problems at all making the three-and-a-half-mile walk.

Sanderson and Davis thanked their helpers and waved good-bye as the officers drove them away. The two men continued on, taking the route Albert Dyer used to flee the murder scene back to his shack in Inglewood.

The men walked briskly but not too fast that they might call attention to themselves, as they assumed Dyer had done. They took LaBrea to Eucalyptus Avenue, down to Beach Street and then on down to Commercial Street to Coop's barbershop—about another hour. Coop would testify that Dyer stopped there sometime between 5:00 and 5:45 on June 26.

They would work out the detailed numbers later—time to various positions along the route with the girls, estimated time Dyer would have spent in the canyon, and the time the WPA chauffeur claims he saw Dyer on the road leading away from the Baldwin Hills. The important thing for now was that Fitts could show jurors how the walk was possible and that Mrs. Mitzutani and Mr. Reilly really did see those children walking to their deaths that day. And he would show that Albert Dyer was the one leading the way—a sinister "Pied Piper," as some newspapers were calling him.

MARIE'S CLASSMATE FROM elementary school, Howard Hilborn, told me the police approached him and some friends to see if they would do the experimental walk. He said the police were asking a lot of kids and everyone knew about it. Howard said his group, and a lot of other boys, had been more than willing but at the last minute, the officers changed their mind and used the young girls instead.

I always think of my dad tucked safely away with friends or relatives during so many of these scenes, but he was still in Inglewood and he must have heard about the walk. It must have reminded him again of the whole horrifying business, a predator posing as a crossing guard, his sisters killed violently in a remote canyon, far from help. And no matter how deep down you bury something like that, it has to surface—at least sometimes, which I think it did.

Most of the time, my dad loved people and books and music and good food and fishing and so many other things. And everyone seemed to love him because he was usually funny and animated, and, like his brother Carl, quite handsome. His smile was electric. But he was also incredibly strict and sometimes turned sullen for no apparent reason. My sisters and I lived with constant curfews and inexplicable, arbitrary rules about manners and conduct and schoolwork. It was impossible to be good enough. He was similarly hard on friends and deemed them worthy or unworthy, using criteria unknown to any of us. Boyfriends didn't stand a chance. He absolutely forbade any of us girls to get our ears pierced before we were eighteen, telling me when I pressed him, "You don't want to call attention to yourself when you're so young."

But something was behind his endless rules and regulations, and it always felt to me more like he was being protective rather than mean or harsh. He would tell us, "It's not that I don't trust you, it's that I don't trust other people—the cruel world and all the crazy people in it."

I once zigzagged through a grocery store parking lot, walking right by a van—the old mostly windowless Econoline type that I'm sure every parent of a daughter feared. My dad pulled me aside so quickly, right there, and sternly told me to never ever walk by a van like that. "That side door can open and someone can pull you in before you ever know what hit you." I was only about ten years old, but I still remember how he hugged me right after he'd given me that warning. No, honey, you didn't know any better, but please don't ever do that again. The world starts to look a lot different—a lot more terrifying—when your dad, your protector, points out potential danger at every turn, and even a hug doesn't bring full comfort. But it makes sense now. The crime against his sisters and Jeanette Stephens changed the way my dad, and so many people, looked at the world.

I'll never know how the murders affected my dad beyond him being so strict with me and my sisters, and maybe causing his unexplained sadness at times. Again, he named his first daughter after the two girls, so he was obviously able to enjoy their memory and wanted to keep it alive to some degree. But I can't be sure about anything else. He never talked about it. I suspect he put the tragedy away deep inside somewhere and tried to live outside that place, until it drew him in again so as never to be fully forgotten.

IT WAS A gray, overcast day in 2015 when I rounded the corner from Centinela Avenue, left onto East Hazel Street. The quaint little homes were mostly gone, nondescript stucco apartment buildings in their place, cars parked everywhere and not a child in sight. Doubtful that anyone living there knew of the history, of what happened all those decades ago. There seemed absolutely no connection between that neighborhood and my family's life.

But then I approached the end of Hazel Street and saw the odd tri-section of Hazel, Marlborough Avenue, and Warren Lane, a place my aunts and uncles, and my dad, must have crossed countless times. And there, right across the street, Centinela Park—or today, Edward Vincent Jr. Park. It too didn't look anything like the scene from 1937, but it was disturbing being there, knowing it was the place where that dark day began. I didn't linger long. Just couldn't.

Around the park—all the street signs I'd read about, Centinela, Florence, East Redondo, Prairie. And just on the other side of the park, Inglewood Park Cemetery, where Jeanette Stephens is buried.

Up Marlborough Avenue, I passed the intersection with Brett Avenue, where Albert Dyer often worked as a crossing guard. Then up ahead, the girls' school—Centinela Elementary School—the outside seeming relatively unchanged and timeless in a way the park wasn't. I could see Marie and Madeline skipping up the sidewalk to the welcoming little buildings, their teachers no doubt waiting at the doors for another day of discovery. I swung by the site of the Hazleys' old place on Stepney and a few other landmarks, all unrecognizable so many years later.

Then back to the park to retrace the walk—and to feel whatever I might feel.

Pulling out onto Centinela Avenue, leaving the park, I thought about how they left that summer morning and never came back. But time marched on and here it all was, nearly eighty years later, teeming with people and bustle and no essence of those lives lost.

Centinela to Market Street, then over to Forrest, to Fairview and up Overhill Drive to Slauson, then west on Slauson to the intersection with LaBrea and up to the Baldwin Hills. So many hills and dips and turns. Even if the girls on the experimental walk made it all that way without a problem, it must have seemed long—or maybe not, because they knew they were with protectors, police officers following closely, right there to take care of them. If my aunts walked that route and had any inkling they were in peril, or even if they started worrying because they were doing something so out of the ordinary, getting so far away from home, it would have been excruciatingly long.

But as I drove it and took in each block, I knew nobody could have enticed three little girls to make that kind of trek, especially not the oldest, Marie, who just talked the night before with her mother and older sister about not going anywhere with a man. No. That walk never happened.

EVE OF TRIAL

Los Angeles County Jail
August 5, 1937

ISABELLE DYER WAS facing her thirty-second night in the Los Angeles County Jail. She had a slight cold and she was so tired. She told the jail matron who looked in on her that she might let her hair grow long because it would be pretty. She knew Albert's trial started the next day but she wouldn't be there. They'd told her she wouldn't have to testify; it would be too hard on her. The lawyers knew she couldn't be compelled to testify against her husband anyway, but even if she agreed to bear witness against him, no one at the DA's office wanted the jury to hear her testify, because she tended to ramble on about the strangest things, like growing her hair long or naming the scrapbook she created "Marge." They'd think she was crazy, too, and worse yet, they'd think the prosecutors were cruel for putting her on the stand.

In another jail cell, Albert Dyer paced and stared, and smoked incessantly. The two suicide watch guards were looking forward to the officers who would relieve them in a few hours for the night shift. Watching Dyer was exhausting. And the trial hadn't even started yet.

THE PEOPLE OF THE STATE OF CALIFORNIA V. ALBERT W. DYER

California Superior Court, Los Angeles, California
August 6, 1937

THE CROWD STARTED gathering at the Hall of Justice before 6 a.m. Husbands and wives, mothers and fathers, sisters and brothers, aunts and uncles, all bound by the collective horror of the deaths of the three little Inglewood girls. Women were in their Sunday best, hats and gloves and spotless white shoes to match their handbags. The men were in their suits and ties, their nicest hats in hand. Five hundred people jostled nervously hoping for one of the 150 seats inside the Department 45 courtroom.

Newspaper reporters and photographers were swarming. Los Angeles County Sheriff's deputies were out in force, ever-watchful for any signs of trouble brewing. They rested hands on their holstered guns, jumpy from the sounds of flashbulbs popping every few seconds.

About 9:30, bailiffs showed Mr. and Mrs. Everett through a side door and into the front row of the gallery. Dyer's foster mother, Etta Young, came in a few moments later and was seated on the opposite side of the courtroom. Deputies opened the main doors at 9:35 and the attorneys arrived at their respective counsels' tables at 9:40.

And at 9:55, a side door opened and guards escorted Albert Dyer into the courtroom where he would answer to three counts of first-degree murder. The courtroom went still, all eyes on Dyer. He was not handcuffed. Guards removed his heavy hand and leg manacles just outside the door to the courtroom. He was unconsciously rubbing his left wrist. He was wearing a shirt and tie, and some slacks, no belt, with his hair smoothed back. He looked much older than in some of his newspaper photographs, where he'd always had a kind of youthful five o'clock shadow and disheveled hair, and where he was always smiling. But now he seemed disoriented by the scene, not sure where to look. Guards gathered around him and helped him to a seat next to his attorneys.

Merle Everett did not react as he watched the man accused of killing and mutilating his little girls. Dyer was only fifty feet away.

Judge White finally entered through a door behind the bench, as the bailiff thundered, "All rise! The Superior Court of the State of California is now in session, the Honorable Thomas P. White presiding. God save the State of California and this honorable court. You may be seated."

As Judge White was taking the bench, fifty of the eighty prospective jurors were arriving at the Hall of Justice and being taken to a room where they would wait to be called to service.

Judge White called the proceedings to order and announced the case.

"People versus Albert Dyer."

Deputy DA Simpson: "The People are ready."

Deputy Public Defender Neeley: "The defendant is ready."

Judge White spoke mechanically as he looked down, surveying the documents and files his clerks had arranged for him on the bench.

"Let the record show the defendant is in court with his counsel, Deputy Public Defender William B. Neeley, Deputy Public Defender Ellery E. Cuff, the People being represented by Chief Deputy District Attorney William E. Simpson and Assistant District Attorney Eugene D. Williams. You may draw a jury Mr. Clerk."

White wasted no time instructing the bailiff to bring in the first twelve potential jurors. And so began the age-old process of questioning jurors, known as voir dire, Old French for "to speak the truth." The process took time and patience, but it was a powerful tool to pick the right people and to foreshadow arguments. The attorneys teased with bits and pieces of their case, asked potential jurors questions designed to uncover bias or predisposition, which was a significant concern in Dyer's case because the details of his crimes and confessions had been front-page news for weeks, potentially tainting the jury pool far and wide. So, both sides probed carefully.

In particular, the prosecution wanted to test whether potential jurors doubted Dyer's guilt. Simpson asked each prospective juror the same question: "You realize it is not your duty to reach out into thin air for an imaginary doubt in order to free a man guilty of these atrocious crimes, don't you?"

The defense countered with their own question about doubt: "No matter how the other eleven members of the jury voted, if, after carefully weighing all the evidence in the case, and there was a reasonable doubt in your mind, one way or the other, would you be swayed by the other members or would you hold out for your personal judgment?"

The defense previewed Dyer's mental condition and the heinous crimes against the victims.

"There will be testimony offered tending to show the mental condition of this defendant. Some of it will be given by doctors, or psychiatrists, long trained in detecting derangement of a person's mind. Have you any prejudice against such testimony? Will you take that into consideration in arriving at your final decision?"

"There will be photographs of a revolting nature showing horrible details of the crimes for which this defendant is accused. Can you look at those photographs dispassionately and consider them in the cold light of evidence only, or are you so sentimentally constructed that you would be swayed by your emotions?"

And previewing an important and often-confusing aspect of criminal trials—confusing because of a defendant's protection against self-incrimination under the Fifth Amendment and the common defense strategy of not subjecting even a mentally stable and articulate defendant to the perils of cross-examination by the prosecution—the defense warned jurors that Albert Dyer would not take the stand, he would remain silent. "You will not hold that against him?"

Each side tested reactions to their questions, verbal and otherwise, watching how certain ideas landed, or didn't. After weeks of press coverage, the majority of potential jurors were surely hostile to Dyer, but both sides still wanted the right mix to decide the case. They worked all day.

When Judge White finally adjourned court at 4:30 that afternoon, he ordered the twelve jurors who'd made it through questioning into the sheriff's custody for the weekend, under heavy guard at the historic Rosslyn Hotel in Los Angeles. They would be sequestered every night for the duration of the trial. No discussions with anyone, no newspapers, no radio. Selection would begin again Monday, starting at 10:00 a.m.—sharp.

WHEN DEFENDERS NEELEY and Cuff got back to the office that first afternoon, they found more letters from Inglewood citizens who didn't believe Dyer's confession. The letters, like all the others they'd received, were encouraging because of their consistent message from people who knew Albert Dyer, who were sure he was the wrong man, feeble-minded and harmless, a victim of police pressure. But nobody had any hard evidence to support their claims. And evidence is all that mattered. The rest of it was just words.

PICTURES OF YOUR family. About twenty of them.
Of all the photographs from the Los Angeles Public Library, I was moved most by a shot of my grandparents on the first day of Dyer's trial. It was my grandfather's forty-third birthday. Given the courtroom layout and their seats, my grandmother seems to be staring at Dyer. But my grandfather's look is more distant—eyes brimming slightly with tears, jaw resting on his hand, a finger nervously extended to his mouth.

When they got back to the house after that first trying day in court, my grandfather probably stood on the porch as the afternoon shadows grew long, looking over at the park where children were still playing. I imagine my grandmother going out to him, careful to not let the screen door make any noise behind her, and then gently putting a hand on his arm. They stood quietly, silently wondering when—if—things like birthdays would ever matter again.

ON SATURDAY AFTER the first day in court, Dyer pleaded with his jailers to see his wife. "She can help me. I know she can. I want to talk to her." The guards ignored Dyer's pleas and distracted him with offers of more cigarettes.

THE JURY

California Superior Court, Los Angeles, California
Monday, August 9, 1937

JURY SELECTION RESUMED on Monday—a full day—and on Tuesday, Simpson continued the voir dire process by hitting potential jurors hard with previews of the case—nooses pulled tight, bloody clothing, violent sexual attacks, mutilated bodies, the little shoes in a row. He calmly instructed them. As a juror, you must dispassionately weigh the evidence and determine whether the defendant Albert Dyer committed these acts. We will ask you to review the evidence in detail. You will have to relive the crime over and over again.

Suddenly, juror James Alcock, a retired rancher, rose to his feet and cried out. "I feel that I can't stand this. I'm sure I could not stand it if I had to sit here two or three weeks and hear the details of such a horrible crime."

The judge quickly took control. He seated an alternate in Mr. Alcock's place and asked everyone to please concentrate anew. Williams picked up where he left off and with even more intensity. The remaining jurors seemed to be bracing themselves.

Then the day got even stranger.

Dyer laughed out loud in court as one of the prospective jurors expounded at length about his personal theory of the doctrine of reasonable doubt. Then Dyer asked a bailiff for paper and pencil and began taking voluminous notes, leaning forward and back, holding his forehead as he wrote. Everyone was disturbed by his strange behavior and after the morning session, reporters asked again for jailhouse interviews with Dyer, with no success. Neeley and Cuff always kept Dyer away from the press, describing how it was impossible to talk to him. "After we talk to him five minutes he goes so completely up in the air it is hours before he calms down," Cuff explained.

But after court adjourned at 4:30 that day, Neeley and Cuff finally granted reporters access to the accused. Flanked by his attorneys, Dyer proceeded to repudiate his confession a fourth time.

"I didn't do it. I couldn't do such a thing. This is a terrible thing for an innocent man to have to face. The right man will come along some day and really confess to those crimes after I'm dead and gone and then it will be too late to save me. My foster mother took me out of an orphanage when I was four years old and she raised me. She knows I never had anything wrong with me that would make me do that terrible thing.

"Those poor children! I felt terrible when I first heard they were missing. If I had done it you don't think I would have gone out and tried to find them do you?"

"Why did you confess?" a reporter interrupted.

"I was threatened into it. I thought it wouldn't be long until they got the right man. The police all ganged up on me and threatened to take me back to Inglewood. That scared me because everybody there was crazy that night." He began perspiring. He seemed to be trying not to smile.

Another reporter—"Do you want to take the witness stand in your own defense?"

"I sure do and I'll tell my story from start to finish." Dyer then recapped that he was home most of the afternoon of the murders, and "there are plenty of people who know I was. The only thing I really hope right now is that I can keep my wife. I need her and she knows I'm innocent."

Then Cuff interjected, "We are trying to locate Fred Godsey, former Utah convict," and the reporters' scribbling must have come to a stop. Godsey?

"Since we have been assigned to Dyer's defense, we have been trying to locate this man Godsey. It is singularly outstanding that in addition to the fact that his description fitted perfectly with the man first sought and that he performed the many tricks that 11-year old Olive Everett often described, he still remains a mystery man."

The defense team was also interested in Godsey because he drove a "pepped-up" fenderless Ford with a box on the rear, the car that so many witnesses from the park had described. Cuff explained that Godsey sent his wife in Salt Lake City a postcard from Butte, Montana, several days after the murders. He could have easily fled to Butte in that time frame.

Suddenly the impromptu press conference made so much sense.

After keeping Dyer incommunicado for more than a month and everyone wondering why he wasn't taking the stand in his own defense, Neeley and Cuff unleashed Dyer to the press so he could repudiate his confession without the prosecution cross-examining him. If the state's attorneys were given even the slightest crack at questioning Dyer, the results could be disastrous. Any decent prosecutor's first line of attack would be to lead Dyer down the garden path to another confession, but this time under oath in front of the jurors deciding his fate.

Instead, by talking with the press and giving Dyer a chance to deny the crimes, the defense could make it clear that—aside from their legal duties as public defenders—they did not believe their client was guilty. They were looking for Fred Godsey because the police had stopped doing so. Someone had to catch the real killer.

It was important to create reasonable doubt, inside the courtroom and out.

MEANWHILE, THE FINAL jury was still not seated because the battle before the war was on. The state's attorneys had marching orders from DA Fitts "to leave no stone unturned toward seeing that the death penalty is meted out to Dyer." They wanted a "death qualified" jury, people who were not opposed to the death penalty and who could vote for it if they thought it was the correct punishment. Such a panel would almost guarantee that Dyer would hang once convicted. In the hands of the right prosecutor, a death-qualified jury is like a stacked deck.

So, defense attorneys Neeley and Cuff were determined to get a panel who would at least consider the mitigating circumstances in Dyer's case, primarily his mental condition. Neeley explained the concept over and over again to potential jurors.

Mr. Dyer's confessions must be taken with a grain of salt. A mentally challenged person will often admit to things that never actually happened. But because they were so close to the event and the people involved, they truly believed it happened and they tell their story, but their story is a lie.

After enduring three days of these endless lectures and questions from the defense, Judge White was growing impatient. He recalled a *Los Angeles Times* editorial just a few weeks before trial, in which the writer warned against letting the case get mired in a troubled system:

> *Indications already are to be seen that the Inglewood triple murder case may become involved in a legal maze. In this case—of all cases—such a condition should not be allowed to rise. Albert Dyer, the confessed slayer of the three little girls, is entitled to a fair trial. No one gainsays that. But as has been pointed out all along since he made his detailed statement of guilt, there always is the danger of prolonged legal tangles over trivial technicalities and side issues. These ought to be quashed before they start. This is not a matter of the public thirsting for vengeance upon an individual. The very horror of the whole case makes it imperative that inexorable justice be done as swiftly and as calmly as is humanly possible. Only the supreme penalty can write finis to the bloody affair. There should be no maudlin interludes.*

Judge White surely agreed, but it's doubtful he would allow laymen who dwelled in newsrooms behind typewriters to tell him how to run his court. The only interludes—maudlin or otherwise—would be those required under the law, as he alone decided. Nonetheless, the case was ripe for certain technicalities and lingering and no judge under the public microscope of a triple-murder trial would tolerate either for long.

He finally reached his limit at the end of the third day and before adjourning that afternoon, he demanded that a jury be seated the next day, Wednesday, August 11. And he backed up his demand with a threat. If a jury wasn't impaneled the next day, he would hold night sessions until it was.

JEANETTE STEPHENS'S PARENTS couldn't bring themselves to go to court until that Tuesday. But they left as soon as the witnesses were excused when it was apparent jury selection would continue into the next day. Some spectators purposely looked away as Mr. and Mrs. Stephens headed out, while others tried to make sympathetic eye contact. Nobody knew what to do. Nobody could begin to imagine what they were going through.

ON WEDNESDAY THE 11th, the defense heeded Judge White's orders to finish jury selection. The attorneys selected six men and six women and, unlike cases today in which the media is barred from photographing jurors in the courtroom, and in cases that prompt judges to protect juror identities for a period after a controversial verdict (Casey Anthony or George Zimmerman, for example), the newspapers ran a group photograph of the panel and printed each juror's name and address. They would not be able to hide after they rendered a verdict and they were surely aware of that fact.

THE PROSECUTION

California Superior Court, Los Angeles, California
August 11–12, 1937

FINALLY, MIDDAY ON the 11th, the trial got under way in earnest. Deputy DA Williams used his opening statement to tell jurors the horrific story of Dyer's crime, to stir emotions and prepare them to convict a murderous fiend. Williams detailed how the killer systematically murdered each little girl and then assaulted and mutilated their bodies. Williams' revelation that the sexual assaults were post-mortem was the first correction of the early press reports that the girls were "outraged, then killed," but the timing issue could not have lessened the jurors' shock and repulsion, no matter what relief they may have felt that the girls did not have to consciously endure the attacks. The story was horrifying, and Williams was so intense, even Dyer couldn't bear it. After Williams finished detailing the killings and assaults, Dyer began weeping. It was a dubious start for the accused, with the damage only possibly lessened by a huge map in the center of the courtroom that blocked the jurors' view of the sobbing defendant.

Eventually, after what seemed an interminable wait, Williams wrapped it up, and Judge White quickly shifted to the defense. "Does the defendant desire to make an opening statement at this time?"

Neeley wisely declined, knowing the jurors were startled and fragile after Williams's details. The defense would seem insensitive at best and desperate at worst if they began attacking the prosecution and offering a wrong-man theory at this early juncture. Better to not dignify the horrifying details with an immediate response. Better to see just what the state had in its arsenal and then make a more specific opening later about how it was all wrong.

"We do not desire to make an opening statement at this time, but we do desire to reserve the right to make a statement at the time the prosecution rests and the defense proceeds with its case."

But just to be sure, Cuff asked the court to instruct the jury. "Will your honor admonish the jury that the opening statement made by the district attorney is not to be considered by them as evidence against the defendant in any way, shape or form whatsoever, but is only for the purpose that they may keep it in their minds and may better follow the evidence?" Judge White agreed.

"Ladies and gentlemen of the jury, the opening statement of either side, the People having made an opening statement, and should the defendant choose to make an opening statement subsequently, you are to keep in mind that the opening statements of counsel are not evidence in any wise. It is a statement of what they expect to prove so that you may follow the evidence as it is presented to you, but you are not to regard an opening statement as evidence of any kind. You may proceed with the testimony."

The state first called county surveyor Fred Kohl, who established that the crime scene was—depending on the route—about 3.5 miles from Centinela Park. The defense cross-examined Kohl, trying to get him to concede another half mile from the pool area to the point outside the park where the walk began, and they noted elevation changes along the way. The mileage and terrain would be important for them later when they argued that Dyer could not have walked three little girls such a difficult distance. The jurors surely welcomed a break from the gory details of Williams's opening, but the break was short-lived.

Boy Scout Frank Portune then courageously recounted finding Marie's body in the Baldwin Hills. Williams asked him to look at a photo from the scene.

"I will show you now a picture which his Honor has permitted me to mark People's Exhibit No. 2 for identification, and I will ask you to examine that and state whether that is a picture of the body that you saw on the afternoon of June 28th in this canyon."

"Yes, that is the one I discovered."

"Yes. And was it lying in the position that you there see it at the time when you discovered it or saw it?"

"Yes; the head was facing south."

"The head was towards the south and the feet towards the north?"

"Yes."

"And it was lying alongside of the bank in the bottom of the canyon, was it?"

"Yes."

Williams asked Portune to identify each body as he'd seen them that afternoon, and in the process, surely leading the jurors in their minds to the lonely ravine and the remains of Albert Dyer's victims. Then, the little shoes.

"Did you, in addition to seeing the bodies, see some shoes?"

"Yes, there were three pairs."

"Where were the shoes lying with reference to this first body that you saw?"

"They were lying north from the feet."

"Were they in the bottom of the canyon?"

"Yes."

The defense tried on cross-examination to grill Portune about the ravine's narrow and steep terrain and how difficult it would be to maneuver in there, subtly suggesting to the jury that the bodies may have been brought there and arranged just like the shoes, by someone who could carry them in a car or with help. But it didn't work, couldn't work, and all the jury would remember was the image of the clean-cut, earnest Boy Scout recounting his brave service to the community and the horrific discovery that led to this very day.

AS THE PROCEEDINGS were coming to a close that day, a newspaper photographer asked to take Dyer's picture. Cuff and Neeley nodded and gave the photographer the go-ahead. Dyer protested.

"Listen, it's up to me isn't it? Why in the hell are you letting them take so many pictures of me anyway?" he snarled.

Neeley explained, "It's better for you to have a posed picture in the paper than one that may show you to a disadvantage. That's all we're trying to do."

"Oh, okay then." And Dyer resumed posing and smiling for the cameras.

ON THE SECOND day of its case, the prosecution continued to focus on the crime scene. Boy Scouts Albert Portune and Horace Card described the ravine and the aftermath of their grisly find—reporters, police officers, others all trying to navigate the tricky terrain, trying to avoid disturbing the bloodied bodies. Two deputy sheriffs testified to similar matters, one of them outlining how the bodies were wrapped in sheets and carried hammock-like up to the "dead wagon."

But testimony could only go so far in getting jurors to comprehend the horrific acts, so the prosecution next introduced enlarged photographs of the girls' corpses. The photographs were painfully detailed, showing the childrens' distorted, injured faces, their mutilated genitals, Marie's tiny hand clutching at the rope.

The courtroom was silent. The jurors shifted uncomfortably in their seats. Even the male jurors winced at each new image displayed before them. And then juror Shirley Agranoff collapsed.

AFTER A SHORT break for Mrs. Agranoff to compose herself, the prosecution continued to paint the full picture of the triple murder. The physical evidence came next.

The ropes from around the girls' necks.

Deputy Sheriff F. P. Dickerson explained how the autopsy surgeon cut the tiny nooses from the girls' bodies and how if you reconnect the two clean-cut ends, you will see the extremely small loops. Dickerson pointed out hair attached to one of the ropes and concluded that it was Madeline's. And so it went with the other two ropes, as they were passed around to each of the jurors.

The defense tried to stop the momentum—and the stream of macabre evidence—by suggesting they be allowed to dispense with two quick witnesses so they could cross-examine Deputy Dickerson in full the following day, rather than trying to rush it that afternoon.

Judge White agreed and the day closed with Don Oliver and Mr. Stephens confirming that they identified the girls' bodies. It was emotional testimony because they were relatives of the victims, but at least it wasn't as bad as tiny nooses straight from the morgue.

FRIDAY THE 13TH

California Superior Court—Los Angeles
August 13, 1937

IN EVERY TRIAL, momentum for either side usually ebbs and flows from day to day, even hour to hour, depending on a variety of factors, from tangibles like witness testimony to intangibles like an attorney's rhythm and connection with jurors.

Then there are days when the momentum starts in one direction and barrels like a runaway freight train down the tracks to conviction. The prosecution hoped Friday, August 13, would be that kind of day in the case against Albert Dyer. Witnesses were slated to put Dyer in the park, luring the girls away and then leading them in the direction of the hills.

Catherine Craycroft, who worked at the park pool, said she saw the girls just before noon shaking out their blanket as if they were leaving to go somewhere. She had a conversation with them—the one reported in the newspapers about the girls going rabbit hunting—but the exchange was hearsay and the prosecution didn't even attempt to bring it in.

Hugh Flynn testified how the girls checked their things with him—the blanket and a bag with a book, a ball and a teddy bear—but he didn't testify to seeing Dyer in the park.

The Villarino twins, Lily and Violet, both thirteen years old, did see Dyer in the park. They both placed him under the big pepper tree.

Mahlan Goddard, a lifeguard, testified she saw a man "answering the description of Mr. Dyer" just before noon. She spoke with him briefly through the pool fence, but because she was focused on the pool and he was behind her, she didn't get a positive look at him, just a quick glance. But she remembered denim overalls and a crossing guard cap, and when the prosecution produced overalls found at Dyer's home, she proclaimed them to match those she saw "exactly." On cross-examination, the defense discredited her by noting that she later saw Dyer's picture in the paper and identified him at the showup based on the newspaper photo. Still, the overalls were in evidence.

Fifteen-year-old Dorothy Reitz saw him at the pool, first standing behind her and minutes later, to the side, holding a little girl's hand. The girl had blond hair, straight and short. The little girl eventually dropped Dyer's hand and skipped away. "She looked like she was happy." Dyer was wearing denim pants and his white crossing guard cap.

The Japanese store owner, Kaneo Mitzutani, testified through an interpreter about seeing the Everett girls walking north on Centinela between 2 and 3 p.m. She knew the girls and both of them turned back and smiled at her as they passed. She thought she'd seen two or three other people ahead of them, but she couldn't be sure if they were adults or children, male or female.

George Reilly testified about seeing the odd convoy—three little girls with a man up ahead—on Overhill Drive heading toward the Baldwin Hills about 2:30. When asked about the man in the lead, Reilly mentioned that he was about five feet seven, had dark wavy hair, and was wearing light denim pants. Williams noted that Reilly attended the police showup a week later, and he asked if Reilly had seen Dyer there and was Dyer the man on Overhill Drive that day? Reilly confirmed yes, "resembles the man that passed my office." He also observed at the showup Dyer's unique walk—a slight stoop and sort of straightforward walk, throwing the feet—like the man who passed by his office.

But the defense dodged a bullet when they established that Reilly didn't report to police what he'd seen until after Dyer was in custody, until after his picture was in newspapers everywhere. And when pressed about the man he saw pass so quickly by his store, through a series of paned windows, could he say it was Albert Dyer? "I could not."

Then the WPA chauffeur Joseph Field testified about seeing a crossing guard who resembled Dyer coming from the direction of the Baldwin Hills and heading back toward Inglewood at 5:30 Saturday afternoon. Light denim pants, crossing guard cap, so strange on a Saturday evening that far away from town. And yes, Field testified that he'd identified Dyer at the showup. But once again, the defense established that Field never reported what he'd seen until after he'd been following the story about Dyer, and he identified Dyer at the showup after seeing many photos of him in the papers. Neeley worked to create as much doubt as possible by quizzing Field on what he'd seen at the showup, including whether he remembered seeing Neeley and Cuff there. Field couldn't remember much of anything.

Court adjourned. The state had notched some wins, but the defense was still standing, having scored a few points of their own. The prosecution would have the weekend to prepare for a final blow on Monday.

THEY MUST HAVE felt confident going into that final day because they made themselves available to the *Los Angeles Times* on Sunday and previewed Monday's court action. They explained how Monday's evidence would clinch the case, or as the Sunday *Los Angeles Times* headlined it, "Dyer's Description of Gate May Send Him To Gallows."

They would present evidence showing how Dyer described the bean field gates through which he took the girls to their deaths in the ravine. His description of the second gate is the one they hoped would sink the final nail.

On the day of the murders, the second gate was a simple two-strand barbed-wire gate with cloth rags attached to each strand, and they said Dyer described it that way in his confessions. But the next day, when search parties were flooding into the hills, the landowner reinforced the gate by adding three more strands of barbed wire and attaching a heavy cable to the two end posts.

Only someone who went through that gate on Saturday—or before—would have seen a two-strand barbed-wire gate. Dyer could not possibly have seen the gate when he went to the hills as part of the search party on Sunday, as the defense would surely argue, because the gate had been changed. The gate would be a smoking gun.

ALBERT DYER HAD no access to newspapers and so he couldn't possibly have seen the constant headlines about nooses and gallows and the state's tightening grip on his life. He didn't have to read newspapers, though, because he was there, hearing it all firsthand at trial. He was hysterical.

Two days in a row he collapsed in a rage as deputies took him back to his cell from the courtroom. And when they reached his cell, he began wailing and screaming and tried to escape from his guards. Once in his cell, he smoked incessantly and brooded for hours, without food or sleep.

The deputies on suicide watch stepped up their vigilance.

THE STRONG FINISH

California Superior Court, Los Angeles, California
August 16–17, 1937

OUR CRIMINAL JUSTICE system is rooted in the fundamental principle that the accused is innocent until proven guilty, or more specifically, innocent until the state proves him guilty beyond a reasonable doubt. The burden of proof is on the government, which requires the prosecution to present its case first, known as the case-in-chief. If the defense were forced to lead, it would convert the system to guilty until proven innocent—*here, you are charged with three counts of first-degree murder, now prove you didn't do it.*

Instead, the accused is not required to put on a defense at all and defense attorneys are given the significant benefit of watching the state's entire case and then seizing the opportunity, if they need it, to refute the state's evidence and perhaps even provide evidence showing the accused is not guilty. The state then has a limited chance to rebut any efforts from the defense, but because of this time-honored system of due process, prosecutors must finish strong on their case-in-chief, leaving jurors with a strong impression of guilt before defense attorneys try to make a very different impression.

So, it was no surprise that Simpson and Williams would close with their most powerful evidence: the gate, the medical examiner's testimony, and their aces in the hole—Dyer's confessions.

But the morning started out tenuously, with an apparent chink in the state's armor. The gate, with all its media-induced weekend hype, was a nonissue. Admitting photographs of the two gates, the parties stipulated—agreed on the record without requiring further proof—to the two-strand gate being in place on June 26 and the five-strand with an additional cable there on the 27th. No testimony, no analysis, nothing. Perhaps in reviewing one of Dyer's confessions to be used later that day, they saw that he referred to four strands of barbed wire and not two. In fact, in just about every confession, Dyer referred to four strands of wire. The prosecution had apparently lost at least one of its smoking guns.

Instead, they opened by recalling Deputy Dickerson to admit the girls' dresses and the little shoes. Curiously, he informed the court that the shoes were back in his office. The prosecution hadn't thought they were necessary, but Cuff said he wanted to see them and someone was dispatched to get them. In the meantime, the dresses and some underclothes were produced and the jury was walked through apparent blood splotches, dark smears, and other unsettling features. It must have been horrifying.

The shoes finally arrived and the defense took over, in particular confirming that Dickerson turned them over to the LAPD chemist for testing, teeing up a defense closing argument that the chemist was never called to testify about fingerprints found on the shoes.

"Are they in the exact, same condition now with regard to dirt, sand, mud, oil or anything else that may have been on them as they were at the time?"

Dickerson affirmed, "They are."

Wesley Engstrom, an investigator with the DA's office, added more physical evidence to the mix: the denim overalls found at Dyer's home, which were in evidence already, a belt, a pair of white gloves, what appeared to be a small money bag, and a badly soiled handkerchief, the latter being most curious since Dyer had consistently told investigators he used a handkerchief to wipe blood from his body and had burned it at the scene. But the evidence was admitted, with Engstrom testifying that he turned over the items to the LAPD Crime Laboratory for forensic analysis and that the chemist there, Mr. Pinker, snipped out multiple samples of fabric from the overalls where stains appeared—four such snips in front near the crotch, several on the pant legs at the knee and the hem, and one at the front pocket. On cross, Cuff established that Pinker took seemingly endless samples and even kept the full garment, setting up another defense closing argument about Mr. Pinker's glaring absence on the witness stand, where he should have been testifying about his laboratory findings on these items and how those findings connected the accused to the crime.

The press made hay with testimony from the barber Mr. Coop and how Dyer told him on June 28 that he was in a hurry to get to the Baldwin Hills to search for the girls' bodies, but the defense neutralized him with admissions that yes, everyone saw the news and knew the girls were likely dead, with searchers focused on the Baldwin Hills. Coop proved nothing.

AFTER THE SHOES and the clothes, the jurors knew the medical testimony was coming. They were eased into it with Dr. Charles Decker, who examined Dyer's genitals late on July 4 after his first confession. With several witnesses and a stenographer looking on, Dr. Decker used a magnifying glass and found "minute, very minute, tears or scars or marks from tears" on the foreskin of the penis, a swollen and reddened area at the base, and a "pouting" of the urethra opening— features that led the doctor to conclude that the foreskin had been forcibly stretched backward. And for good measure, Decker examined Dyer's genitals again that very morning and while the swelling and redness in one area was gone, the urethra features seemed the same and were apparently normal for Dyer.

Unfortunately for the defense, on cross-examination the doctor emphasized that the alleged crimes would have caused "violent stretching of the foreskin backward." But he also admitted that Dyer's foreskin was unique, so he couldn't even tell if Dyer had been circumcised. But Neeley also got Decker to clearly establish that during his examination on July 4th after the first confession, the room was crowded with only investigators and that Albert Dyer was effectively alone with nobody there to represent or advocate for him.

Two more physicians testified similarly about Dyer's physical condition, concluding that his injuries would not have been caused by "normal" sexual relations.

AFTER THE LUNCH break, the autopsy surgeon Dr. A. F. Wagner took the stand. The jurors braced themselves, but it didn't matter. The prosecution moved immediately to the morgue photographs and placed them on an easel in front of the jury and then stepped away, respectfully, as if at graveside. The jury members had seen them before but were horrified all over again.

The prosecutors needed to connect Albert Dyer to these monstrous images. The jurors must have been thinking, after Dr. Decker's testimony, if Dyer caused those injuries to the girls, why wasn't he injured more severely? How could he possibly cause that kind of harm and not tear himself more in the process?

Simpson approached Wagner and the jurors waited for answers. But Simpson kept them waiting while Wagner enumerated in sickening detail the injuries he'd found on each girl: bruises, lacerations, blood, congested lungs, "a rope tied very tightly about the throat," vaginal and rectal tearing, rape, sodomy.

Simpson asked for more, for the surgeon to please show the jury the nature and locations of the lacerations as they appear in these photographs. Wagner seemed shocked.

"Shall I exhibit this to the jury?"

"Yes."

And he did, pointing out specific areas of injury on each girl, Marie, Madeline, and then Jeanette, describing body parts as being "torn down," "torn apart," and "forcibly dilated." The testimony seemed endless.

Then Simpson dug deeper, asking Wagner if he'd formed an opinion about how the violations were committed.

"I think that the lacerations were not caused by penetration of a male organ. I think that those lacerations I found were formed by the hands. . . ." He suggested that they probably were made by "other means than the natural means" and added that the unique nature of the internal tears was the same on all three girls.

Simpson kept the doctor moving, avoiding a break so the powerful testimony would continue unabated. Assuming the lacerations were accomplished by the hands, there would be immediate bleeding, would there not?

"Yes, it usually results in considerable blood—hemorrhage."

And even with these tears, wouldn't the act result in considerable pain and injury to the penis of the person who violated these girls?

"Not if the openings were forced by other means than that of the male organ."

Simpson didn't need to dwell on the horrifying point any longer. He knew the jurors understood. Albert Dyer tore these girls apart with his bare hands, and then he'd used their blood to lubricate his sexual attacks.

THE CORONER'S TESTIMONY stunned me. How could a human being commit these acts? All I could think about was Fred Godsey, reportedly ripping telephone books in two with his bare hands. His wife saying he was "inhumanely cruel." His friend describing how "pain and suffering inflicted on others meant absolutely nothing to him."

THE CONFESSION WOULD be the next—and most powerful—nail in Dyer's coffin, but the prosecution needed to convince the jury that his statements were voluntary. That meant going back to the private meeting between DA Fitts, Sheriff Biscailuz, and Dyer the morning of July 5, after he'd confessed the night before. Both men testified about being alone with Dyer, telling him they only wanted the truth, that he wasn't being offered anything to confess—no immunity, nothing—so, if he hadn't killed those children, to speak up and set things straight. But instead he'd said, "Before my God I killed them."

The defense made multiple attempts on cross-examination to question the men about why the stenographer wasn't present when he was in a nearby room, and why nobody else was present, and how could Dyer have possibly understood what "immunity" meant? But Judge White sustained every objection and the dubious nature of this purported good-cop meeting would be quickly forgotten as the forty-six-page grand jury confession was read into the record. DA Fitts did the reading from the witness stand, but by the second page or so, the jury was surely hearing Albert Dyer say every word.

When it was finally over, Cuff and Neeley asked to approach the bench. They planned on objecting to the confession and they had witnesses to support that move, to provide evidence of coercion, but the witnesses "were not in the courtroom at the proper time, so we permitted it to go ahead." Admitting this to Judge White and the prosecution must have been excruciating for them—it was either a colossal professional blunder or an inability to control forces with greater influence than theirs, both embarrassing and potentially catastrophic to their case. But they had to do it so they could ask for the right to challenge the confession at a later time. Judge White agreed, saying it was only fair to give the public defender that right. Even Simpson agreed.

In the meantime, the defense would have to expose as much as possible by questioning the man who was with Dyer at so many key moments during the chaos of July 4 and 5. They walked Fitts back through all those hours of confessions, physicians, examinations, and more confessions, always painting the picture of a feeble-minded exhausted defendant with no attorney or anyone else to assist him as the walls closed in. Fitts conceded some technical points, but he was skilled at providing just enough facts to answer the question without giving much away.

At one point, Cuff asked if Fitts subjected Dyer to even more interrogation after he'd confessed twice, but Fitts countered by suggesting he was being quite the friend. "I had a very short talk with him in the restroom while the doctors were making a physical examination. I sent out and got himself and myself a steak."

THE PROSECUTION CLOSED with some loose ends.

The experimental walk, to which the defense objected on every basis imaginable. Neeley argued vigorously that it was impossible to simulate the same conditions as that day, how long the girls were in the park before the walk, who was leading them, and what incentives they may have had. He pleaded for time to brief the law but Judge White said the experiment showed only the possibility of the walk, nothing more, and the jury could decide what weight the evidence carried. The jurors then heard about three little girls who easily made the trip, and who, after climbing out of the steep ravine and into the bean fields, had enough energy to run the last 100–150 feet back to the police car.

And for good measure, they introduced into evidence the white bone-handled clasp knife Dyer referred to in his grand jury testimony. The one he said he used to cut the clothesline rope to strangle the girls.

And just before the midday break, the state rested.

THE CSI EFFECT

2009

WHEN I FIRST told a friend my doubts about Dyer, she said, *Well, they must have been able to match his blood and fingerprints and everything, right?* You would think. They couldn't match everything, and certainly not with the precision we can do so today, but yes, a violent triple murder and multiple sexual assaults should have yielded some evidence that could be connected to Dyer. And yet, there was none.

The trial transcript is just shy of 1,200 pages and more than half—735 pages—are the prosecution's case-in-chief and rebuttal. But no matter how many times I went through it, I couldn't find testimony about the physical evidence that should have been admitted in this case.

Why didn't my grandmother's brother, the LAPD fingerprint expert no less, who announced early that the bodies and shoes had clear prints, why didn't he testify that Dyer's prints were a match? Maybe he was too biased, but didn't anyone analyze those prints? Of course they did. The Los Angeles Public Library sent me a photo of a man analyzing Dyer's prints under a magnifying glass, with documents and materials around him. The newspaper archives are filled with photos of Dyer being printed. And even the FBI ran his prints and offered their analysts to assist.

Also missing was any connection to the mysterious and much-touted candy bag found under Marie's body, evidence that the prosecution reported early on would clinch the case against Dyer. The *Los Angeles Times* reported that the clerk who claimed she sold the bag to

Dyer "has not been located" and she never testified at trial, nor did anyone testify about fingerprints or other physical evidence linking the bag with Dyer.

Where was the LAPD chemist, Mr. Pinker, to testify about Dyer's clothes and his handkerchief? What about all those samples he snipped for testing? If the state found blood on anything and could have made even a remote match to Dyer or the girls, the testimony would have been damning. Where were test results comparing hairs in the ropes and hairs from the goat the two men bought from Fred Godsey? There was nothing.

Instead, investigators testified that yes, they found some overalls, and then showed the ropes he used, the girls' dresses, their shoes, all from the grisly crime scene. *Ladies and gentlemen of the jury, look at these horrific items. Albert Dyer is guilty. Next witness, please.*

The absence of meaningful testimony is glaring.

Ironically, I expected quite the opposite. Problems with physical evidence and flawed or fraudulent forensic testing—"junk science"— have led to many wrongful convictions, especially in older cases when scientific methods for testing blood and fingerprints were relatively rudimentary. So, I thought certainly the state would have put on testimony, no matter how flimsy, and the defense would attack collection and testing methods, exposing the limits of this evidence even by 1937 standards.

In fact, one of the more unbelievable case photos shows several investigators handling bare-handed the tiny nooses and the girls' clothes, with one of them even smoking a cigar over the pile of evidence. You almost expect to see some cold pizza or a sandwich in the mix, so cavalier is the scene. And the Boy Scouts and others testified to chaos in the ravine after the bodies were discovered, footprints everywhere and multiple people handling the bodies. The defense even probed Deputy Dickerson about the lack of blood beneath Jeanette's body, suggesting the crime occurred elsewhere, the ravine a dumping ground. But all these issues were collateral and did nothing to link—or unlink—Dyer to the scene.

Instead, there was no such testimony and no chance to expose anything. The prosecution never even addressed testing of the physical evidence, avoiding altogether any risk of cross-examination from the defense.

All the jury saw and heard was that each pitiful dress and pair of shoes belonged to one of the murdered girls, right where Albert Dyer left them after his unspeakable acts. And here are his pants, denim just like everyone said they were.

Today, most people in our CSI-saturated world mistakenly believe that DNA and other forensic tools have eradicated the possibility of a wrongful conviction. Researchers have even identified a "CSI Effect" that works on jurors who will often ignore overwhelming evidence of guilt or innocence, asking for DNA evidence because it's all that matters. And sometimes it is extremely conclusive, in sexual assault cases, for example. But biological evidence is available in only 10 percent of criminal cases, so DNA is not useful or even present in most homicides, robberies, and burglaries. More importantly, even where it is useful, even the best CSI team can't typically work with contaminated evidence or a crime scene that's been compromised, as was surely the case in Los Angeles in 1937.

Maybe the jury noticed these holes in the state's evidence. Maybe nothing mattered because they'd already made up their minds when it was time for the defense to make their case.

THE DEFENSE

California Superior Court, Los Angeles, California
August 17–19, 1937

THE STATE PUT on a strong case. And because the defense had no affirmative evidence of innocence—no airtight alibi, no conclusive eyewitness testimony, and no indisputable forensic evidence—they would have to, as one newspaper put it, "break down the state's groundwork." To save Albert Dyer, they would have to create reasonable doubt by bringing back Eddie the Sailor and the mysterious Ford roadster, by putting Dyer in Inglewood at the time of the crime, and by casting Dyer's confessions as the product of police pressure on a vulnerable suspect who had no idea what was happening to him. They opened by introducing jurors to the police officers who first applied those pressures.

Neeley questioned LAPD officer R. O. Williams about arresting Dyer early on July 4, the two-hour interrogation in the parked squad car near the city dump, and the drive to the Baldwin Hills. Officer Williams confirmed that during that first interrogation, Dyer denied having anything to do with the murders.

Staying with the chain of police custody, Neeley put Lieutenant Sanderson on the stand to recount how Dyer next arrived at the Inglewood jail, was questioned for an hour until about 4:30 and how he continued to deny any involvement in the crime. They'd then moved Dyer to the Hall of Justice and resumed questioning him that evening, just a little before 8 p.m. Neeley exploited the obvious time gap that would have given police time to work on Dyer.

"By the way, do you know in whose custody Albert Dyer had been during the period from the time you left him in Inglewood until you saw him at the Hall of Justice at 7:50?"

"Yes, in the custody of Detective Lieutenants Williams and Chandler; at least, that was the instruction given."

"So far as you know, he was?"

"So far as I know."

But somehow, just twenty minutes after the new interrogation began in Los Angeles, Albert Dyer confessed to the murders. Neeley wanted to confirm that this very first admission came after the three-hour gap and so quickly after the second interrogation began.

"That is the first time?"

"Yes, sir," Sanderson replied.

Rather unbelievably, this line of questioning would open the door to yet another reading of Dyer's confession. On cross-examination, Deputy DA Williams wanted to clarify the time line and statements Dyer made on July 4 by having Sanderson recount everything in detail. Neeley and Cuff protested but to no avail. *Objection overruled. You may proceed.*

The confession seemed to go on forever.

The defense countered by calling two witnesses who were at the Hall of Justice on July 4 and 5 to testify about post-confession photos that ran in the major newspapers. Dyer is near collapse, exhausted, looking absolutely confused and overwhelmed. In one *Los Angeles Times* photo, he is actually lying down with officers attending to him. The defense's message was simple—investigators worked hard on Dyer for ten hours. They wore him down. Anyone would have confessed. *Any one of you jurors would have confessed under that kind of pressure.*

Then the defense moved the court to strike all of Dyer's confessions as involuntary. But the judge refused and reserved his ruling until the completion of the case. For the defense, it meant more time for the damaging confessions to sink in with the jurors.

Another blow for Dyer's side came with R. E. Perry, a local real estate man with a large-windowed office facing Centinela Avenue, testifying he was there all afternoon and never saw Dyer, whom he knew, walking by with three little girls or otherwise. Deputy DA Simpson handled the cross-examination.

"What were you doing there that afternoon?"

"Sitting around waiting for prospects mostly."

"How many other people passed your office that afternoon that you did not see?"

"Well—"

Cuff: "I object."

Simpson: "That is all."

NEXT UP WAS Russel Hawthorne, the park's popcorn stand operator and one of Haskell Wright's group who'd adamantly maintained since the beginning of the case that Dyer was the wrong man. He'd known Dyer for two years. He'd seen a different man doing rope tricks for a group of children.

But Hawthorne couldn't say whether the Everett girls were in the group of children being entertained and the point seemed to be lost.

Worse, Hawthorne testified that he'd previously identified a photo of a man he believed he saw in the park that morning—probably Strong or Godsey. But when Neeley tried to go down that path, asking who provided the photo, the state objected and the judge sustained. Conversation over.

Harry Loescher operated the sweet corn stand at LaBrea and Slauson and was there all day on the 26th with a full view at least a half mile in all directions. "I did not see a man or children walking past my stand on that day."

Twelve-year-old Florence Frailey reported before trial that she saw the girls leaving the park on foot with a man who was not Dyer. But the spotlight of the witness stand got to her and she fell apart when the prosecution pressed for details. Cuff tried to save her on redirect—by questioning her again after the prosecution's cross-examination—and while her final answer indicated she did not know the man she saw, the damage was done and the jury must have felt sure she was coached.

SHIFTING GEARS, THE defense worked to bring back the other man who had a car, with their witness William Emery testifying about seeing an old stripped Ford in front of the park that morning. The driver was not Dyer. But the prosecution asked to cross-examine Emery later and when they brought him back, they asked him if he'd ever been convicted of a felony.

"Yes, sir."

The prosecution: "That is all."

The felony turned out to be forgery. It was not a violent crime that would cast Emery in the same lot with the likes of Dyer, but it was a crime of deception that compromised Emery's credibility as a man claiming to be telling the truth. As a result, his valuable eyewitness testimony likely meant very little to the jurors.

John Rouard, a former deputy sheriff who lived across from the park, provided a little counterbalance. He was an established lawman and he echoed Emery's testimony. He'd seen a man doing rope tricks that morning and then later saw the same man pushing an old Ford in front of Rouard's home. Three little girls were in the car.

Charles Atkins owned a shoe repair shop near Dyer's home and talked with him many times. Atkins saw Dyer on the 26th about 5 or 6 p.m and noticed nothing unusual about him.

THEN, BACK TO the park and one of the defense's most anticipated witnesses. Ten-year-old Lillian Popp was playing with the girls that morning when a strange man approached and asked them to go rabbit hunting. The girls said no, but when he promised ice cream and candy, they finally agreed. The man who talked to them, and the man with whom the girls left the park, was not Dyer, and she would know because she attended the same school and Dyer was her crossing guard, too.

But under cross-examination, she added that all three girls had bathing suits with them, a fact that was never reported anywhere. Further, Lillian didn't know about the girls having a shopping bag they later checked with Mr. Flynn before they left the park. She couldn't remember anything about it. She'd also never seen Dyer in the park, contrary to so many others who testified about seeing him there regularly. The bathing suits and shopping bag were cheap distractions from compelling testimony, but the jury would be left wondering if young Lillian knew what she was talking about.

Equally disappointing was Kenneth Hylander, who'd noticed a man under a big pepper tree, with two little girls playing nearby on the lawn. Good. The defense began to set the scene a little more for Hylander, referring to a blanket under the tree—the blanket Marie and Madeline brought that morning. But Hylander couldn't recall and when Neeley pressed him, he seemed uncertain and almost defensive.

"Well, for the purposes of refreshing your recollection, did you tell me just about twenty or thirty minutes ago that there was a blanket there nearby where that man was lying?"

"No, I did not."

"Did you on last Saturday, in Centinela Park, tell me that that man was lying on a blanket under the tree?"

"I might have said that."

"Well, tell us your best recollection whether or not there was a blanket there where this man was lying."

"I would not say definitely if there was or not."

"What is your best recollection?"

"There was, that is my recollection."

And the man on the blanket was not Albert Dyer, but it may have been difficult to believe that recollection when Hylander couldn't even remember the blanket in the first place.

MARGARET RIGBY, WHO lived three doors down from Dyer, testified she saw him at 1:30 on Saturday picking up papers in front of her house. Rigby was also prepared to recount seeing a scratched and bloody man—not Dyer—run through the vacant lot next to her home between 4:30 and 5:30 p.m on the 26th. But the prosecution blocked the testimony because the man was three or four miles from the crime scene with no possible connection. Neeley argued vigorously about the time frame, how the killer would have been on his way from the scene. The judge saw no evidentiary value whatsoever. Objection sustained.

The barber, Claude Coop, testified for the prosecution but the defense pitched him as one of their witnesses, exploring what Coop saw on Sunday the 27th, when he and Dyer hoed weeds in Coop's yard for about two hours. If Dyer's genitals were as injured from the crime as the prosecution claimed, he could not have worked so hard and long. Coop agreed he hadn't seen any scratches or bruises on Dyer, and he hadn't noticed Dyer suffering from any pain or anything out of the ordinary.

Henry Turville of the LA *Examiner* called on Dyer at home about 5:50 p.m. and collected money for a month's paper delivery service. He even produced a receipt.

Dr. Benjamin Blank was the Los Angeles County Jail physician, and when he examined Dyer on July 5, he found no injuries, abrasions, or inflammation apparent on Dyer's genitals. But the prosecution was able to glean that Dr. Blank had not used a magnifying glass.

Emma Robinson, Dyer's former landlady, said he and Mrs. Dyer visited her home from 1:00 until 1:20 that day. Dyer, in his confession, put the time of the murders at 2 p.m.

Then a break from witnesses as the defense read another confession into the record, a confession in which Dyer couldn't even be consistent about whom he murdered first and other simple facts—he drove ahead of the girls, no, he walked with them, he strangled them with his hands, no, it was rope, no, it wasn't rope, it was binder's twine, and more. The inconsistencies were troubling.

Dr. Glenn Meyers, a psychiatrist hired by the defense to examine Dyer, was a strategic follow-up after the obviously confused confession. Dyer had the mentality of an illiterate nine- or ten-year-old boy. His memory was not reliable—he couldn't repeat back even a six-figure number with any accuracy. But despite defense efforts to further exploit the mental challenges, Meyers would not attest to Dyer having any "special suggestibility."

They came at it from another angle, asking Meyers to opine about false confessions, and what type of person might be prone. Meyers explained that some people may develop a deep sense of guilt during childhood, for example by wishing their father dead—a somewhat common childhood thought—which they then push to their subconscious. But when they learn later in life that killing is wrong, they compensate for the guilt by, for example, "being unusually kind to people."

The testimony was lost on everyone. Rather than a discussion about how someone with limited mental capacity could be prone to suggestion through leading yes-no questions, the examples and conclusions seemed random and irrelevant.

Neeley quickly changed course by asking if Dyer, with his low intelligence and the emotional effects of the trial, could assist in his defense. Meyers replied he could do so only to the extent a nine- or ten-year-old child could.

But Meyers's testimony lost steam again when the prosecution asked him what the average mental age of American troops was in the First World War.

"I don't remember exactly, but it was around twelve to fourteen, and there were certain group tests that were used, and—"

Mr. Williams: "That is all."

And one final attack on Dyer's confessions. He'd confessed once that after the murders he started a fire to burn his blood-soaked handkerchief and the fire got out of control. Another time, he'd said he dropped the handkerchief in a smoldering campfire that he later snuffed out. Lloyd Louterborn, an oil company inspector in the Baldwin Hills, reported seeing signs of a fire only on Sunday night. There were no fires large or small in the Baldwin Hills on Saturday.

THE ONLY THING left for the defense was their Hail Mary—the motion to strike the confessions. They cited the long interrogations, the leading and suggestive nature of the questions, the defendant's low mentality, and how all these factors led to an act that was coerced either by physical violence or continued questioning. Judge White disagreed.

"I am satisfied that all that the People are required to do is to show that the confession was freely and voluntarily made, without any hope of reward, offering of immunity, any force, violence or duress, and possibly the court might be called upon to determine whether or not the mental capacity of the defendant was such that he understood the questions asked and the nature of and purpose of the answers he gave thereto." But even so, it would be up to the jury what weight they would give to the confessions.

Motion denied.

CUFF AND NEELEY lost some important points. Still, they'd resurrected Eddie the Sailor and the Ford, and they'd marshaled a host of people willing to testify in support of Dyer despite the potential perils of doing so in such a small community and on such a public stage. The jury would conclude these witnesses must be telling the truth and were trying to save a man they knew was innocent. They'd also exposed Dyer's troubled and challenged mind in a way that could lead the jury to conclude that he was not a crazed killer because he couldn't even count to eleven. Perhaps it would be enough.

But apparently they decided they needed more, and the next day they made a motion to take the jurors to the Baldwin Hills, presumably to support their argument that wiry little Albert Dyer, with his nine-year-old mentality, couldn't possibly have murdered three children and disposed of their bodies in the complicated gulley maze.

Prosecutors Williams and Simpson must have wondered what on earth their defense counterparts were thinking. They'd gain nothing by going to the ravine except stirring jurors' imaginations, making them visualize the scene, the three little girls, the assaults, Dyer arranging the little shoes. They would take in the inhospitable landscape and grieve again for the girls who met such a ghastly fate so far away from home. They'd see the deadly ravine all night while locked up at the Rosslyn Hotel, in their dreams and again in the days that followed, and certainly in the jury room during deliberations.

The next day Judge White said no. Dyer had a constitutional right to go to the scene because, with judge, jury and attorneys there, it was his trial and under the Sixth Amendment to the US Constitution, the accused is entitled to attend the proceedings, wherever they may occur. But Judge White cited security concerns, refusing to expose the jurors, everyone, to the potential dangers of having a notorious defendant back at the scene of the alleged crime. People with their own brand of justice would surely be waiting for Dyer there.

Another motion denied.

And then, just two weeks after the opening gavel, the defense rested.

REBUTTAL

California Superior Court, Los Angeles, California
August 19, 1937

IN REBUTTAL, THE state had one more chance to counter the defense and to seal Albert Dyer's fate before the case went to the jury. They began by trying to disprove the defense allegations that Dyer was coerced into confessing.

They called on four men who were with Dyer on July 4 and 5, all explaining why he appeared slumped or collapsed in newspaper photos. Flashbulbs were scaring everyone and Dyer cowered a little, so they carried him to the restroom for his physical examination. At the booking window, photographers asked him to pose this way and that, and he did—every time. But he was fine. Didn't seem fatigued or tired or upset, unless he was talking about the actual killings and then he cried.

The most curious of these witnesses was Captain Winn, an assistant chief of the DA's investigation unit, clearly brought in to close the three-hour time gap before Dyer confessed the first time. Winn testified that officers Chandler and Williams brought Dyer to the Los Angeles Hall of Justice about 4:45. Winn observed Dyer until 6:45 when Winn went to dinner, and then when he got back at 7:30 until the time Dyer was booked hours later. He testified that nobody questioned Dyer and that, in fact, Winn instructed guards to not allow any questioning. Dyer was fine, smoking and talking with people, never forced. Calm and rational.

Dyer's attorneys, and perhaps the jurors as well, must have wondered: why weren't officers Chandler and Williams testifying, or the officers who guarded Dyer during those three hours? Officer Williams had testified earlier, so why not bring him back for a first-hand account? Or why didn't Winn testify during the case-in-chief, avoiding the suspicious time gap? Dyer denied committing a crime for most of the day and then suddenly, after sitting alone in an office for several hours, he cracked after twenty minutes of interrogation. That was the story.

The state also had the last word in the battle of experts, a common strategy when a defendant's mental state is at issue. They tried to neutralize defense witness Dr. Meyers with seven doctors of their own. In testimony that was tedious and sometimes terrifying, they related Dyer's low mental capacity, his version of the crime, and his sexual history and preferences, including his recent desires for girls younger than his wife.

The doctors all read from notes taken when they met with Dyer—not stenographer's notes, but their own. And they all recounted Dyer giving detailed narratives about the crime, explaining certain points, elaborating on others. Suddenly, in these private meetings, no more yes-no answers and a lot of vocabulary that Dyer never used during other questioning.

"The little girls, Marie, Jeanette and Madeline, went to the swimming pool attendant and told the lady there they were going rabbit hunting, but she did not think anything of it, she thought they were going to chase rabbits in the park."

Detailing the sexual assaults, he uses the word "rectum" and explains, "I waited about an hour between these acts."

On being in the ravine: "I knew where they were. The Boy Scouts found them, I did not tell them. I was with the crowd, I was among about fifty people. I helped carry one of the girls, it was Madeline, to the hearse. I got a trembling feeling inside myself and it was not a sexual desire."

But Dyer was still confused about which girl he murdered first.

He told one doctor he "felt sorry" and wanted probation.

He told another that "any man who would have done anything like that should be hanged."

The testimony was curious. Dyer saying he felt sorry and wanted probation in response to being charged with first-degree murder or that the murderer should hang absolutely refuted the idea that he was acting rationally. The defense objected repeatedly but the testimony went on, and the jury's last impression would be multiple doctors who believed Albert Dyer was the killer.

THE DEFENSE SEIZED the last word though—reopening the case after the prosecution's rebuttal to bring in newspaper photographer Harold Muldoon and to admit two photographs showing that Dyer was with him while he closely photographed the bodies at the scene. Muldoon confirmed Boy Scout Frank Portune's testimony that Dyer had ample opportunity to see the bodies, just like so many other people in the ravine that terrible day.

Maybe the final effort would help. Maybe not.

"It looks bad. It looks bad," Dyer told one of the guards back at his cell after court adjourned. "It looks really bad."

CLOSING ARGUMENTS

California Superior Court, Los Angeles, California
August 23–24, 1937

IN THE END, the defense made a surprisingly strong case for Albert Dyer. A good closing argument should remind the jury about every question and inconsistency in the state's case. A skilled defense attorney will make jurors ask themselves: *With a man's life on the line, how can I be sure?* And Neeley and Cuff did just that. They spent nearly four hours over two days walking the jury through their arguments.

Dyer denied any involvement for ten hours. Only after he was moved to the DA's office and apparently left alone—or worse—for nearly three hours did he admit anything. And he was inconsistent about key facts. Dyer's confessions were yes/no answers to leading questions, and the inconsistencies are understandable when a man is trying to retell a story planted in his feeble mind by police interrogators. Neeley condemned the prosecution for "explaining away things that did not fit into the story because, they said, his [Dyer's] memory was faulty."

Cuff shored up Neeley's efforts, disclosing to the jury that "Dyer's accounts of that tragedy were so garbled that it was difficult for his questioners to make head or tail of what he said. This garbling with him is natural, the result of a mentality of an eight- or nine-year-old child. He himself was the greatest obstacle to his own counsel because of this.

"The prosecution attorneys, officers and others attempting to solve the triple murders at no time tried to get him to give an account

179

of what he did on any day other than the day of the murders—except on one occasion. And this occasion brings before us a vital point, and one which I think you should weigh carefully.

"When the DA's investigators asked Dyer what he did Friday night before the murders, Mr. Dyer said 'why, Friday, I went downtown and sold papers. They said a woman was thought to be the kidnapper.' But ladies and gentlemen, the children were not even missing at that time."

When investigators departed from the script, Albert Dyer didn't even know what day it was.

The defense solidified the incapacity argument with a final image for jurors: "Imagine a nine- or ten-year-old child being brought to the Hall of Justice and facing all of the investigation and questioning the defendant encountered prior to those confessions." They hoped every juror would imagine a son, grandson, or nephew surrounded by detectives, the walls closing in.

And what about Eddie the Sailor, doing rope tricks, flipping his wrists back, and inviting the girls on a rabbit hunt? Remember Lillian Popp. Even though she'd been confused about the bathing suits, she was right there; she saw Eddie.

"This was a child who knew Dyer well. She had played that morning in the park with those three little children who were later murdered. She was there when they were invited by this strange man to go on a rabbit hunt. They left with him. And she said that man was not Dyer."

And the prosecution's witnesses only speculated on what happened that day. Yes, they may have seen Dyer in the park, but he was a crossing guard near there. Talking to children he had known for some time does not mean he later killed them. The state hadn't connected any dots.

What about the mysterious fenderless Ford, the two witnesses who'd seen the children leaving in it? Where is this man Fred Godsey, who could throw his wrist out of joint at will? This man who played on the blanket with the three murdered children in the park before they disappeared? The girls could not walk that far, just as the Everett parents doubted early in the case. The prosecution's experiment didn't prove anything.

Dyer knew things about the murders and the condition of the bodies because he was in the ravine when the bodies were found.

Equally troubling was the absence of his wife, Isabelle Dyer, who could not testify that Dyer was in his garden on Saturday because the state was holding her as a material witness, protecting her from any threats of harm or tampering.

Neeley confided in jurors that "If it were possible to have brought her before you, I haven't any doubt but that, if she were normal minded, she would have remembered that Dyer was home all during the afternoon during which the State contends he murdered Madeline, Melba Marie Everett and little Jeanette Stephens." The jurors could picture a wife desperate to save her husband, but held by the too-powerful and unfair forces of the state.

Finally, most powerfully, the lack of physical evidence and no testimony whatsoever about fingerprints or blood from Dyer's clothing, nothing connecting Dyer to the knife or the ropes the prosecution introduced. Cuff had previewed his arguments in the press the day before, declaring "Those shoes were undisturbed until detectives took charge of then. The killer handled those shoes in taking them from the feet of his victims and arranging then in the order they were found. There should have been prints on them, but not a word of testimony concerning any prints was offered."

The prosecution established the violence with which the children were sexually attacked and yet physicians, the county jail physician as well as a doctor appointed by the prosecution, testified they found no evidence of injury, abrasions, or inflammation on Dyer's genitals.

Then on Tuesday morning, Neeley and Cuff wound up their case with a bold move.

"The State has failed to prove its case against Albert Dyer!" Neeley shouted to the jurors. "You must acquit him of these charges.

"I am asking you to take into consideration that you are trying a human being with the body of a man but only the mind of an undeveloped eight-year-old boy." And of course, Albert Dyer didn't take the stand in his own defense because, like a child, he is so susceptible to suggestion and leading questions—as evidenced by his confessions—that the prosecution could make him say anything. Prosecutors Williams and Simpson know this. The State's evidence is of an exceptionally unstable nature and you cannot send a man to his death based on such evidence."

The prosecutors must have been shocked. *Acquittal? The defense can't be serious.*

Rather than the defense conceding their client's guilt and groveling for life imprisonment instead of the noose, as one would expect in such a difficult case with multiple confessions, Neeley and Cuff went all the way. They pleaded with the jury to find Albert Dyer not guilty. Up until that moment, the jurors probably didn't even think such a verdict was an option. Neeley wanted them to understand that it was the only option.

"There is reasonable doubt and you must find Albert Dyer not guilty."

The courtroom was in stunned silence as Neeley made his way back to counsel's table and took his seat next to Dyer.

AFTER A SHORT recess, Williams took the stage for the state about 11 a.m. on August 24.

"The issue in this case is did Dyer do it? The evidence is so overwhelming against this man that I find it difficult to say anything more. I shall overlook those sordid features which would arouse our emotions and might have a tendency to keep us from being unquestionably fair. We have the most complete and convincing evidence it is possible to have, and it will be only the high spots that I will touch upon."

It was the age-old argument—*a mountain of evidence exists; I won't waste your time reviewing it all.* The jurors would then imagine two or three more pieces of unspecified evidence for each one that Williams actually talked about, whether they remembered the evidence or not. And predictably, Williams started with the confessions.

"It is inherent in human nature that people do not admit wrongdoing unless they are guilty. Dyer did not admit these horrible crimes once, but on many occasions. Nine times, the record shows, and he seemed to get relief from his mental tortures by recounting the events of that bloody afternoon in a lonely ravine in the bleak Baldwin Hills.

"But it is not alone upon these confessions which we have depended for the solution of this infamous crime. We have evidence which you have heard, that is, in our opinion, proof beyond a shadow of a doubt that he was the fiend who lured those innocent children to their doom in those hills." Then the specifics.

Witnesses placed Dyer in the park, possibly en route to the murder scene, and possibly leading away from it. Dyer was holding the hand of a girl who looked like one of the victims. The police walked three little girls from the park to ravine with no problems. Dyer's story of that long walk was not only entirely plausible, it was the truth.

Dyer told his barber on Sunday he had to hurry to the Baldwin Hills to help search for the girls' bodies when no one in Inglewood knew the girls were dead.

Dyer described the gate that was there the day of the murders but gone the next.

And a week after the murders, Dyer's genitals still showed signs of recent tears and other effects consistent with the attacks on the girls. He'd described to Dr. de River how he tried out certain sexual acts with his wife and then reenacted them after he killed the girls. Their blood excited him.

"It's an absurdity to consider anything but a judgment for death for this defendant. Albert Dyer has damned himself for the murders of these three little girls with his nine confessions to the crime."

BOTH SIDES GAVE the jury powerful evidence and issues to consider. But in the back of their minds would be the one fact that neither side could argue away. For more than two weeks jurors watched Albert Dyer, in the flesh, just across the courtroom.

He was only five feet four and about 122 pounds—the type of stunted man who might prey on children because he was too weak and small to take on an adult victim. He was dark, sullen, moody, and erratic. He was squirming, smiling at strangers and talking to people at inappropriate times and places. He once pouted in open court because his foster mother offered him candy instead of bringing him cigarettes. He behaved just like Dr. Meyers described him, like an illiterate nine-year-old boy.

The jurors may have missed some of these particulars by trying to avoid even looking at him, but no matter. Dyer was not a sympathetic defendant. He could look sad and afraid like a child, but he very often looked frighteningly like the sadistic pedophile killer Simpson and Williams made him out to be.

And perhaps more damaging, he'd said nothing in his own defense. His silence wasn't evidence of his guilt, as Judge White would inform the jury in his final instructions, but counsel was permitted to comment on it and the prosecution took full advantage of the opportunity to do so.

Before wrapping up the state's closing, Williams pointed a finger at Dyer: "This man has sat day after day in this courtroom and heard himself damned as the ruthless and fiendish killer; heard himself condemned by his own voluminous statements, yet he has not offered one word to indicate those statements are not true.

"You ask why we are brought here in the face of his many confessions. We are here because it is written in our law that every culprit, even a fiend, must have his day in court. So, we are here and we have vainly waited for his answer to these charges. What has it been? Silence.

"What calls us here? Because that man, Albert Dyer, a fiend in human dress, murdered and violated the bodies of three tiny children. Those murders were the work of a fiend incarnate. Dyer strangled those children with ropes. Those murders were premeditated. Why were they premeditated you ask? Their ravished bodies revealed an unbridled passion, an insatiable lust, that was the motivating power that drove this inhuman wretch to his horrible deed."

The attacks were relentless.

Dyer muttered to himself. Beads of sweat broke out on his forehead when he heard deputy Simpson say he was "eternally damned" for murdering those children. He leaned toward his attorneys, his tongue licking his upper lip. His hands closed and opened every time Simpson read a charge against him.

Then finally, his torment was over. Simpson wrapped it up. *Ladies and gentlemen of the jury, you must find Albert Dyer guilty.*

The case was ready for the jury.

THE CHARGE

California Superior Court, Los Angeles, California
Tuesday, August 24, 1937

A JUDGE'S INSTRUCTIONS to the jury, known as "the charge," should be a detailed roadmap for their deliberations. A judge defines the universe of possible verdicts and narrows the field of inquiry. The charge is critical. And Judge White certainly knew it.

The defense and prosecution both submitted proposed jury instructions. Judge White reviewed them carefully, accepting some, rejecting others, and modifying portions as he saw fit. The final instructions went on for nearly thirty pages.

He was clear from the outset. The jury had only three options for defendant Dyer: death, life in prison, or acquittal and freedom.

"There is no proof in the case of any kind or degree of homicide other than murder in the first degree. Your verdict, therefore, should be either that the defendant is guilty of murder in the first degree or that he is not guilty." The only theory for Dyer's innocence was that he wasn't there; he was the wrong man. Guilty or innocent, nothing in between.

"The defendant is charged in the indictment with three claims of murder which constitute three distinct offenses. You are the sole and exclusive judges of the weight of evidence and the credibility of witnesses. You must arrive at a conclusion without resorting to anything outside of the facts and circumstances brought out by the evidence. A witness willfully false in one material part of his or her testimony is to be distrusted in others." The defense had probably lost Lillian

Popp, who fouled up her testimony with nonexistent bathing suits and a shopping bag she couldn't remember.

"It is the sole duty of the jury after an asserted confession has been introduced in evidence, to determine the truthfulness of the facts and matters contained in said confession and to weigh and determine what credit or effect shall be given to it." The confessions were fair game and the jury must decide if they believed Dyer's admissions. But Judge White gave them further guidance.

"Evidence as to the mental capacity of the defendant at the time he made certain statements or asserted confessions has been offered and received. This evidence is received only for the single purpose of assisting you to determine whether at the time of the defendant's asserted confessions, admissions, declarations and statements concerning the death of the three persons named in the indictment, and his participation therein, charged to have been made by him on July 4, 5, and 6, 1937, he had sufficient mental capacity to remember and relate the matter concerning which he is said to have spoken." The question was not whether Dyer was insane at the time of the crime—no insanity defense was asserted. The question was whether an illiterate and limited nine-year-old boy with a feeble memory could have made those statements. It was up to them to decide.

And finally, the weight on their shoulders. "If you find that the defendant is guilty of murder in the first degree, it will be your duty to fix the penalty of death or confinement in the state prison for life. If the jury should fix the penalty as confinement in the state prison for life, you will so indicate in your verdict. If, however, you fix the penalty at death, you will say nothing on this subject in your verdict, nor will you specify the death penalty in your verdict. In the exercise of your discretion as to which punishment shall be inflicted you are entirely free to act according to your own sound judgment." In other words: *We understand you don't want to play God with someone's life, so we won't make you order the defendant's death. Instead, your silence will allow the law to send him to the gallows.*

At 3:30 p.m., Judge White gave the case to the jury. The bailiff escorted them to their quarters above Judge White's chambers and locked the door behind them, their secret work awaiting. Albert Dyer's life and justice for those little girls was now in their hands.

DID THE JURORS have any doubt about Albert Dyer as they filed away? After all of it, the photographs, the testimony, and the bizarre, smiling monster at the defense table, did they ever wonder if he was the right man?

Did they think about Eddie/Freddie the Sailor? Did they wonder whether Dyer could have committed the murders on his own? Did they think he was insane?

One thing is certain, Dyer's confessions would be powerful evidence in the jury room and if they believed even part of his admissions, they could not possibly acquit him.

And perhaps they felt a more subtle pressure to convict him. The Dyer jurors had been fully exposed at the outset when the local newspapers printed their names and addresses. If they acquitted Dyer, they would be freeing a man many believed was guilty. That fact must have loomed large over them, as if they faced their own judgment day.

DELIBERATIONS

Inglewood, California
August 24–26, 1937

JURY DELIBERATIONS ARE perhaps the strangest part of a criminal trial. After a seemingly endless stream of daily news, testimony, facts, developments, shifts and countershifts, the information spigot constantly wide open, the panel is cloistered and everyone—the attorneys, the families, the public, and most importantly, the media—enters an abrupt and indeterminate communication blackout.

The newspaper coverage of Dyer's case after it went to the jury was reminiscent of so many jury verdicts anticipated and experienced in the collective consciousness: O. J. Simpson, Michael Jackson, Scott Peterson, Casey Anthony, and George Zimmerman, to name a few. We all wait and wonder: what will they decide? What are the victims' families going through? What will this case say about our society, our criminal justice system, our future as a community? The waiting can be excruciating, or in the media's case titillating. And so it was in August 1937.

The jury deliberated for two days, and newspapers tried to keep everyone on the edge of their seats with front page headlines.

The *Los Angeles Times* reported on August 25 that the panel, after deliberating only several hours the night before, was already deadlocked 9 to 3, apparently over the penalty issue. They went to dinner and were "ordered locked up for the night at 10:30 p.m." Tensions ran high and one juror argued with a sheriff's deputy about wanting to make a phone call, which the deputy would not allow. The August

26 front page of the *Los Angeles Times* informed the readers: "Dyer Case Jury Deadlocked; May Be Dismissed Tonight: One Reported Holding Out Against Eleven."

And the jury revealed its issues. They'd gone to the judge twice on the 25th asking questions. First, did Dyer ever identify any shoes belonging to any particular child? They thought the answer went to his mental capacity. The judge ordered relevant portions of Dyer's confessions read in open court. They even brought Dyer back from his cell to hear the jury's questions.

The jury returned to court again later that day and asked if they could decide the penalty based on Dyer's mental state. Judge White instructed they should consider evidence of the defendant's mental state only for the limited purpose of evaluating the confessions, just as he'd admonished in his lengthy instructions. They could not base a finding of guilt or innocence solely on the issue of Dyer's mental state, but they were clearly struggling with convicting someone who was so obviously impaired.

They also asked for a large map depicting the scenes at the ravine. They were still wondering about the long walk.

At the end of the jury's second visit to court, the judge polled them and confirmed they were hopelessly deadlocked 11 to 1. They revealed their standing as to number only, so no one knew which way they were going on guilt or penalty. The jury was burdened with the tall order of deciding both.

Meanwhile, my grandparents and the Stephens family faded into the background, out of the media's reach. Maybe they had long ago turned the whole thing over to the justice system and God, retreating to their privacy, knowing that if Albert Dyer killed their children, he would be convicted and suffer the punishment.

Still, they must have been watching and waiting in those final hours. The reports of the jury's questions—if they knew about them—must have made them wonder. The shoes? Could this man go free because he didn't know which shoes belonged to which child? Dyer's confessions were so muddled, how could one even decide what he knew about the shoes or anything else. The map? Deadlocked?

Then finally, they would have heard that the verdict was in. The DA's office probably sent a police officer with the news. *Come to the courthouse as soon as you can.*

THE VERDICT

California Superior Court, Los Angeles, California
Thursday, August 26, 1937

THE JURORS FILED into the crowded but silent courtroom at 10:45 a.m. Albert Dyer, who appeared without a tie—a standard safety precaution for a man likely to be hearing his death sentence—stared, but not one of them made eye contact with him. They stared at anything but him. They took their seats methodically and once they were all in the jury box, they looked only at Judge White.

"Have you reached a verdict?" he asked.

"We have," answered foreman James Kelley.

Jurors Dorothy Deel and Shirley Agranoff began openly weeping. Mrs. Deel visibly shook as she tried to control her sobs. Judge White called for order. He addressed the courtroom.

"You ladies and gentlemen here exemplify a firm type of Americanism, a type that makes for respectable and decorous conduct. You have shown a proper solemnity in conduct in this trial. Now when the verdict is handed down, I hope you will not by word or act outrage the solemnity of this occasion. I hope you will show the proper respect and remain quiet during all stages of these proceedings. Now Mr. Foreman, you may hand the verdict to the bailiff."

Bailiff P. Putney took the envelope from Foreman Kelley and handed it to Judge White. He studied it for several minutes and then handed it to the court clerk.

"Will the defendant please rise," Judge White instructed.

Dyer and his attorneys stood up. Neeley and Cuff looked directly at the clerk. Dyer continued staring at the jurors.

Then the clerk began. Dyer clenched his fists.

Count I. Murder of Madeline Everett. "We, the jury in the above-entitled action, find the Defendant Guilty of Murder, a felony, as charged in Count One in the indictment, and find it to be Murder of the First Degree."

The rope, pulled tight to a two-inch circle around her neck, silencing her forever. Her favorite Mickey Mouse book lying open and battered in the dirt.

Count II. Murder of Melba Marie Everett. "We, the jury in the above-entitled action, find the Defendant Guilty of Murder, a felony, as charged in Count Two in the indictment, and find it to be Murder of the First Degree."

Her hand clutching at the noose.

Count III. Murder of Jeanette Stephens. "We, the jury in the above-entitled action, find the Defendant Guilty of Murder, a felony, as charged in Count Three in the indictment, and find it to be Murder of the First Degree."

Her bloody torso and legs left exposed in the heavy brush. Her head resting on her outstretched arm.

AFTER THE VERDICTS, the courtroom remained still and quiet, save for Mrs. Deel's and Mrs. Agranoff's stifled sobs.

The families must have felt paralyzed.

Eugene Williams and Bill Simpson must have breathed a quiet sigh of relief; *yes, Albert Dyer is guilty.*

Neeley and Cuff. Perhaps they weren't surprised, but the disappointment must have hit them hard, knowing a man's life had been at stake.

Albert Dyer showed no emotion whatsoever.

The clerk ended the silence. "The jury hereby makes no recommendation for the penalty for the above-referenced offenses. The verdict is duly signed by the foreman Mr. Kelley."

The jury did not vote for life imprisonment. Dyer would hang.

Bill Neeley tried one last maneuver, hoping to tease out any jurors who may have been strong-armed, or who might, after this emotional climax, want to change their minds. He spoke quietly, "Your Honor, the defense requests that the court poll the jury regarding their verdicts."

Judge White could not have been surprised in a capital case of this magnitude. "The clerk will please poll the jury for the record," he instructed.

The clerk asked each juror, "Is this your individual verdict?" and "Is this your individual verdict as to penalty?" And one by one, they answered yes. They spoke softly; the two women jurors still crying labored to speak at all. But with these final answers, the trial was over.

Judge White quickly thanked the jurors for their service and set the matter for sentencing on August 31. He gaveled for adjournment and the courtroom began to stir.

Dyer remained standing with Neeley and Cuff at his side.

As everyone filed out of the courtroom, Dyer leaned in to his attorneys and asked, "What does first degree mean?"

OUTSIDE, REPORTERS JOCKEYED for position as the jurors left the courthouse. They swarmed on foreman James Kelley. He stopped angrily. "We have agreed to make no statement concerning our verdict."

Dorothy Deel, still crying, said, "We made a pact among ourselves to make no comments." And she made none.

"If the foreman won't talk, neither will I. I've been through hell and back again in many situations, but this ordeal was the worst of my experience," proclaimed Charles Truax, a retired naval explosives expert.

The reporters continued to lob questions at the jurors.

Foreman Kelley was furious. "See my lawyer. I want to get home."

Dorothy Deel broke down again. "Why don't you let us alone, haven't we gone through enough already?" she sobbed.

Finally, the press relented, and the jurors hurried away to waiting family and friends.

Back inside the jury room, reporters found scraps of paper. Most had "death" written on them, but a few said "life." A drainpipe in the room was stuffed with other scraps, in an apparent attempt to hide evidence of the deliberations. It seemed Dyer's guilt was never even an issue. Only the penalty.

THE PRESS CONFERENCE.

District Attorney Fitts: "The verdict returned against Albert Dyer was a proper verdict under all the circumstances of this case. The brutal murders and mistreatment of those three children by Dyer constitute one of the most horrible crimes in California history. His case was ably presented by Mr. Neeley and Mr. Cuff of the Public Defender's office. Their conduct was highly ethical and able."

Neeley and Cuff: "We still stand by our original declaration to the jury that whatever their decision might be, it would be accepted by us without comment. We did all we could. We presented the evidence as we saw it and questioned the prosecutions' evidence wherever we thought it was questionable. We did our duty as best we could."

AS THE CROWDS dispersed outside the courthouse, Albert Dyer was arriving back at his jail cell. Still unsettled by the fast pace of the morning's events, he asked his guard, Deputy Sheriff Cecil Luskin, "I won't have much trouble getting probation will I?"

A FEW DAYS later, Isabelle Dyer finally consented to see Albert. He'd been asking repeatedly to see her before he was transferred to San Quentin's death row, and sheriff's deputies eventually gave in and arranged the meeting in the tenth-floor dental office of the county jail building.

Dyer was waiting for her in his jail denims. Deputies brought Isabelle in and Dyer immediately went to her, embracing her. She shrank from his advances, but he lifted one of her arms over his shoulder, trying desperately to make her return the embrace. Isabelle let it fall back to her side.

"I wonder what's happened to the cat," she asked, looking away.

"I guess the neighbors have taken care of it," he said.

As Albert handed her a picture of his foster mother, Etta Young, she asked, "What am I going to do about the bills?"

"You'll get another $11 WPA paycheck."

Isabelle looked to one of the guards who'd brought her there as if to say, enough, let's go. But then she asked the guard, "Will I see him again?"

"Not for a long, long time," the guard answered.

Albert lunged at her, grabbed her in his arms, and kissed her. Again, he took her hands and tried to force an embrace, but she pulled away and her arms dropped to her sides.

"Well," he stammered and choked, "I—I'll—see you in heaven."

Isabelle's eyes filled with tears and she fled from him, back down the corridor with her attendants. But at the end of the hallway, she turned back for one last look at him, at her Albert.

IT WAS THE end of the road for Isabelle Dyer too. DA Fitts alerted authorities at the Sonoma State Home in northern California that he had their escapee. She was returned to the hospital's custody.

ABOUT THIS TIME, reports started surfacing about trouble with young Mike Huerta, who told police early on that Dyer was the crossing guard in the park who'd been trying to lure little boys to hunt rabbits with him. Huerta never testified at trial and instead went missing for nearly a week the day after Dyer was convicted, prompting more suspicions about his early involvement in the case.

THE NEXT DAY, Judge White denied the defense motion for a new trial.

"A review of the evidence in this case and a review now of the rulings and the reasons which actuated the court in the making of those rulings convinces me, and I am of the opinion that this defendant was fairly tried and that he was justly convicted. The motion for a new trial is, therefore, denied. You may stand up, Mr. Dyer."

Dyer stood in his brown trousers, white shirt, and a curiously loud red-checked necktie. He looked a little pale and kept wetting his lips but otherwise did not look like a man about to be delivered to the noose.

"It is now the judgment of the Court and sentence of this Court that for the offense of murder in the first degree, as set forth in Count I of the Indictment herein, you suffer the penalty of death, such penalty to be inflicted within the walls of the State Prison of the State of California at San Quentin, at a time to be fixed in the Warrant of Execution; that for the offense of murder in the first degree, as set forth in Count II of the Indictment . . ."

Dyer seemed to lose interest after the first count and glanced around the courtroom, which was empty compared to during the trial. The only family member in the courtroom was Frank Carey, Jeanette Stephens's biological father, who was long ago divorced from her mother. No one had known about him or whether he'd been coming to the trial. Dyer eventually turned back to the bench.

". . . you are remanded to the custody of the Sheriff of the County of Los Angeles, State of California, to be by him, within ten days from this date, delivered into the custody of the Warden of the State Prison at San Quentin for execution of this sentence. It is so ordered this 31st day of August, in the year of our Lord, 1937."

And the gavel sounded for the last time in the matter of The People of the State of California v. Albert W. Dyer.

DYER'S SENTENCING WAS not only the last chapter of his case in Judge White's courtroom. It was the last time a man was sentenced in California to death by hanging. Effective the next day, September 1, 1937, the condemned would be sentenced to die in the state's new gas chamber instead of in the noose. But the gallows at San Quentin would be maintained and ready for anyone like Dyer who had been sentenced before September 1. In fact, California did not retire the gallows until 1942 after hanging its last man, Robert "The Rattlesnake Killer" James. He'd been sentenced in 1936, but appeals delayed his execution another six years.

THE OWL

Los Angeles Station, California
Evening, September 4, 1937

THE TRAIN PULSED and steamed as passengers boarded and engineers readied for the trip north. It was impossible to escape the news that condemned killer Albert Dyer was leaving that night for his one-way trip to San Quentin's death row in a Pullman car attached to the Southern Pacific Owl that ran between Los Angeles and San Francisco. More than 2,500 people turned out on the platform to catch a last glimpse of the notorious killer.

It was a law enforcement nightmare with the huge crowd. They'd tried to transport Dyer three days earlier but the train was crowded and there wasn't room for their special detail. Dyer told reporters he was happy for the delay.

"I like it in jail here. I get swell treatment!" he quipped happily.

But the delays were over, and Dyer was in the anteroom shackled to three other men also bound for San Quentin. LAPD Sergeant Dan Crowley searched Dyer and did one final patdown before allowing him to finish dressing for the trip. Dyer started putting on the same loud, red-checked necktie he wore to his sentencing, but then quickly pulled it off, unfastened his shirt collar, and started caressing his neck and throat, reporters musing that maybe he was thinking about the noose that awaited him.

The inspections complete, Crowley, Los Angeles County Sheriff's Captain Bill Penprase, and the other two officers walked the men to the waiting train. Dyer made one last statement to Los Angeles reporters and the gawking crowd, screeching over the din as he was hustled along, "I'm still innocent, I'm still innocent!"

Deputy District Attorney Williams was one of the last to board. He was going to see this one all the way to the end of the line.

At 6 p.m., the Owl chugged slowly away from the station.

WHEN SOMEONE DIES, a family is usually swept up in a swift current of making arrangements and receiving family and friends. Then everyone leaves and they are alone with their loss for the first time. And for anyone who's been there, that's often the worst part.

It's hard to know exactly what the Everetts and Stephenses went through. First the search, then the bodies, then the funerals, which were so tangential on July 2 and July 4, almost nonevents compared to the drama unfolding as Dyer became a suspect and then a confessed killer. But rather than holding close to the sanctuary of their homes, they were forced into the next phase of their nightmare, to the criminal charges, the grand jury proceedings, and finally the trial, and all the media attention that went with it.

And the guilty verdict was cold comfort. Yes, Albert Dyer would hang, but my grandparents and the Stephens family would still have to go back to their homes where their children once lived and played. They would have to start rebuilding their lives, or whatever was left of them, while they waited for Dyer's appeal and his possible date with the gallows, when the barely healed wound would open anew.

The news that Dyer left Los Angeles and was on his way to death row must have been, for these families, like that moment after everyone leaves—that moment when time really begins marching on.

CONDEMNED ROW

San Quentin State Prison, San Quentin, California
September 1937

ALBERT DYER WAITED for his date with the gallows on San Quentin's death row—"Condemned Row," they call it there. He must have been terrified.

He'd never done any serious prison time. He had been in jail for vagrancy, but nothing could have prepared him for death row at the bleak fortress on the northern California coast. After he was processed, stripped of his identity, and transformed into Inmate No. 60804, guards escorted him through the Row's infamous barred door and down the corridor that housed some of the most notorious killers in history.

Edward "The Fox" Hickman, who had kidnapped, killed, and dismembered little Marion Parker in Los Angeles just a few years earlier, awaited his date with the gallows there, as had Gordon Stewart Northcott, the man who kidnapped young boys, held them captive on his Riverside, California, ranch, and then beheaded them as if he was slaughtering chickens—the subject of the 2008 movie *The Changeling*.

The men on Condemned Row followed the unspoken law that killers are "brothers under the skin." Death row prisoners were all confined to their cells for twenty-three hours a day so it was close quarters in an antechamber of death and despair isolated away on the top floor of the north cell block. The only other inmates close to them were locked behind solid doors in solitary confinement, an

200

equally horrible section just across the corridor from the Row and known only as "Siberia."

Escape was impossible. The killers' brotherhood was all any of them had.

But the brotherhood didn't include men who preyed on children. Men like Hickman, Northcott, and now Dyer were shunned and outcast in a place where even the slightest sense of belonging was the only human contact available. Dyer was totally alone. And he would have to stay alone. He was a marked man, like all inmates convicted of preying on children, and the death row brothers would tear him to pieces for his misdeeds if only they could get at him.

He deteriorated quickly and steadily, just as the men at old Coop's barbershop in Inglewood feared he would if he was ever locked up somewhere, although they had a sanitarium in mind, not death row at one of the roughest prisons in the country.

Guards reported that Dyer never read anything for the entire year he awaited execution. He wrote letters to his wife and others when he first arrived, but, by November, his foster mother and a purported friend were writing the prison expressing their concern that he'd stopped communicating so abruptly. Etta Young wrote concerning "my son," saying that she had been "receiving 2 to 3 letters per week from him up to November 19, 1937." And in her replies, she was enclosing postage, so she and others worried something must have happened to him.

Instead, guards reported, he only chain-smoked and paced, day after long miserable day. He was let out into an enclosed exercise area for an hour a day but he did nothing there but pace and sit. His endless hours were punctuated only by an occasional meal, which he ate with no interest whatsoever. Sleep was rare and fitful. As his execution date drew near, guards reported that he muttered incoherently during what little time he did sleep. They visited his cell every twenty minutes on suicide watch.

MISTER X

Inglewood, California
October 26, 1937

HASKELL WRIGHT NEVER stopped believing that Albert Dyer was the wrong man, but after the conviction and sentencing, his protestations were just that, with fewer and fewer people caring to listen.

But on a late October morning, a man walked through Centinela Park, and Wright knew immediately he was the man Wright saw doing rope tricks for the girls the day before they were kidnapped. Wright summoned a police officer and they confronted the man. His name was Carl Jensen.

He said he lived in nearby Lennox and was a minister of the gospel and a workingman. He was in the park because his wife's car broke down nearby and he was going to help her. Wasting no time, the officer asked him where he was on June 26, 1937, and, by Wright's account, the man began trembling and shaking, yelling several times "You can't pin that on me." Wright also claimed that Jensen lunged at Wright, but the officer took charge and suggested they all go to the chief of police. The chief questioned Jensen for a bit but ultimately let him go—he was not reopening the Everett-Stephens case.

But Wright would not rest.

A few months later, he consulted with an Inglewood attorney, Ralph Evans, and pled the case for Dyer's innocence—citing all the people who knew Dyer but had seen a different man with the girls that morning. He told Evans about Jensen, the possible "Mister X" in the Dyer equation. Evans thought the issue was worth investigating and recommended that Wright get sworn statements from everyone and then Evans would go from there. Wright launched into action.

He started with park employee F. C. North and William Emery, who had testified at Dyer's trial about seeing the girls in the old Ford roadster. He drove them by Jensen's home and when they stopped in front, Jensen came out to investigate. North said Jensen was the man he'd seen in the park on Friday, and Emery thought the old Ford in Jensen's yard was the car he'd seen on Saturday.

Wright needed to get more witnesses over to Jensen's and conveniently for him, the couple next door despised Jensen. The woman was Mrs. Jensen's sister, and her husband had committed suicide over her having an affair with another man, Tom Gregory. She was now living next door with the adulterous Gregory, Jensen didn't approve of their lifestyle, and the three were estranged. It's unclear how Wright connected with Gregory, but he did, and Gregory offered up his home—with a perfect vantage point to view Jensen—as an informal showup venue.

Wright seized the opportunity, taking Lillian Popp, her cousin Amy Lancey (the girl who'd claimed to have seen Fred Godsey in the park before and after the murders), and Russel Hawthorne multiple times to view him. Wright, with Gregory's help, even set up a fake meeting with someone Jensen believed was interested in buying one of his old cars. The meeting forced Jensen out of his house and into full view of Wright's witnesses, who would all identify Jensen as the man doing rope tricks in the park on Friday and Saturday. His voice was especially damning, loud and hoarse, just as everyone remembered it.

Another voice in the call to save Dyer was Mrs. Rigby, his neighbor who testified at trial about the bloody man passing her window the evening of the murders. Wright took her to see Mister X and while she wasn't as sure as the others, she said his general features were the same as the man she saw on June 26 and his walk—apparently a unique "pull and shuffle"—was exactly the same.

In her sworn statement, Rigby also offered a story about Dyer that Wright's group hoped would call his confessions into more serious question. In September before the crime, there was a car accident near Rigby's and Dyer's homes, and a woman was badly injured. After the ambulance took her away, Dyer told Rigby he didn't mean to hurt the woman, how he could have avoided her if he'd driven more carefully and braked sooner. He was almost crying and the way he told the story, Rigby said, if she hadn't known Dyer, she would have believed he actually did it. She admonished him, told him he was making a "great big story" out of something that never happened and he finally admitted that he'd only imagined he was driving the car. Dyer had concocted the fictitious tale somewhere in his troubled mind.

Evans took sworn statements from all the witnesses, and also from Popp's and Lancey's mothers about June 1937 and the recent visits to Jensen—referred to as Mister X in the affidavits. Meanwhile, Wright involved another attorney, Speaker of the California Assembly William Moseley Jones, who also took statements from these and other witnesses.

The statements brought back to life all the doubts everyone expressed after Dyer was arrested—we know Dyer and he was not the man with the girls. The details are familiar, the moustache, tattoo, dark complexion, dark hair, the rope tricks. But the Lanceys also accused the police of threatening little Amy and her family if she didn't identify Dyer after he was first arrested. Amy stated in her sworn affidavit:

> *They yelled at me and told me "If you don't tell the truth we will lock you up in a dark room and leave you there." When they were asking me questions all the time they pushed my chin way back and held it there and they pushed my hair way back. One of the policemen said he was going out after a big leather strap to beat me with and then he came back and said he couldn't find the strap.*

Mr. and Mrs. Lancey stated in their affidavit that officers threatened to take their children away because they were not responsible and were not taking proper care of them.

While Wright worked to compile a case for Dyer, a newspaper floated a new theory for Olive's molestation charges against Wright during the early days of Dyer's case—and the mysterious way those charges evaporated without explanation. The reporter wrote that because Wright refused to identify Dyer, the police forced Olive to make the accusations to get Wright to comply. But character witnesses had defended Wright and the police backed off—charges were never filed.

THE APPEAL

The California Supreme Court, Sacramento, California
December 22, 1937

WHILE HASKELL WRIGHT had been trying to save Albert Dyer by gathering evidence on Mister X, Dyer's attorneys were hard at work trying to save him through a completely different process—by appealing their client's conviction to the California Supreme Court. The appeal was compulsory, required by law in any case where the defendant was sentenced to death. It was a critically important review, a check on the ultimate punishment before the irreversible was carried out. But just as Dyer's defense team was understaffed and underfunded during trial, they were underequipped for the appeal as well.

Vercoe had to ask the high court for more time to file his opening brief, in which he would have to present the strongest case possible on paper alone, laying out the case, detailing what went wrong at trial, and why Albert Dyer should not have been convicted. Unlike at trial, where the prosecution presented their case first, on appeal, the defense—as the appellant, the one appealing—would get the first chance to convince the justices about Dyer.

The opening brief was so crucial that Vercoe pleaded with the high court in an affidavit filed just days before Christmas in 1937, explaining how the trial transcript was more than 1,200 pages, and his office had 344 other cases set for trial in October, November, and December of that year alone, three of them murder trials. Only eight deputies were available to handle the caseload. He needed thirty more days, but only thirty.

"I assure your Honorable Court that no additional time will be requested for the filing of said brief." It was the lawyer's way of saying, *I know I shouldn't even be asking, but the situation is that bad.*

The Supreme Court said yes. So did the Los Angeles County DA's office. The prosecutors surely doubted that more time would help Vercoe and his team.

But it may have. To be sure, their brief was a shotgun approach, countless pieces of wet spaghetti thrown against the judicial wall in hopes that something, anything might stick. But they raised a lot of questions. Unfortunately, they were questions they had already raised at trial.

When appealing, an attorney must focus on issues of law the trial court may have gotten wrong, rather than asking an appeals court to retry a case by reviewing the evidence all over again. The time to create reasonable doubt is at trial, not at an appeals court. But that's just what Vercoe and Neeley tried to do. They asked the court again and again to look at the evidence and to give Albert Dyer another chance.

And they started in the right place—with the confessions. Albert Dyer has a child's mind. He was interrogated for ten hours. Of course he confessed. And he was wrong about so many facts; he was reciting a script that he hadn't quite memorized. I wanted to supplement their arguments with all the scientific research we have now on false confessions, all the exonerations showing how people admitted to something they never did. But Vercoe and Neeley didn't have any of that history with which to work.

They revisited other closing arguments from trial. No witnesses had put Dyer in the park with the girls and the two witnesses who said they saw the girls later—store owner Mitzutani and real estate man George Reilly—never identified Dyer as being with them. The experimental walk—the evidence should never have been admitted. The lack of physical evidence. Dyer's only alibi was his extremely feeble-minded wife who couldn't possibly testify on his behalf.

Then one new angle—Dyer's genitals. The prosecution cannot have it both ways. Doctors conceded that Dyer showed only minor abrasions, certainly not the kind of injuries expected from such violent attacks on small children, and further testimony from the autopsy surgeon indicated the attacker mutilated the girls with his hands. Dyer never, in any of his alleged admissions, said he'd sexually attacked the girls with his hands. The prosecution also argued that the abrasions doctors found were consistent with a more traditional sexual attack, with no tearing by hand before, in which case Dyer would have been severely injured in those early hours and days after the crime. Instead, he worked in Coop's yard for several hours on Sunday morning, he was in the search parties in the Baldwin Hills and he never showed any apparent pain. Albert Dyer's physical condition did not wash with the evidence.

And finally, multiple legal arguments about how the defense was improperly limited in their ability to cross-examine prosecution witnesses while the prosecution was given relative free rein to cross-examine defense witnesses and to present improper evidence, such as Dr. de River's controversial rebuttal testimony about Dyer's private sex life.

In the copy of the brief I obtained from the California Supreme Court, someone—presumably a clerk but perhaps a justice—placed large, emphatic checks next to only four of the seven legal arguments in the main table of contents, as if they stopped reading them after number four. I thought how difficult it must have been for anyone to have slogged through those arguments, with endless references to the record and procedural rules, after reading all the opening pages filled with descriptions of murdered children, sexual assaults, and confessions. The legal arguments were surely considered and analyzed, but the first impressions must have stayed with everyone as they reviewed the case.

And, of course, the prosecution would be heard, by filing its reply brief and rebutting the defense's claims, making its own case for why they had gotten it right and why Albert Dyer must hang for his crimes. But they didn't take the defense bait to argue the case again in their brief and for the most part, they stuck to issues of law, all of which they disposed of rather handily. On one of the points, the state noted, "This rule of law is so elementary that it needs no further argument or citation of authorities here to sustain the ruling of the trial court." In other words, they would not even dignify the defense's argument with a response. You can almost hear the Supreme Court justices mumbling "yes, exactly" as they read. Check mark.

The state didn't ignore the issue about the confessions, though. Fitts strung together a sound argument that Dyer's confessions were voluntary. The record did not show that anybody threatened or induced Dyer to talk. And while he may be mentally slow, the judge instructed the jury to take that into consideration when weighing the confessions. Fitts cited case after case to support his position, including one where a trial court allowed the confession of a man who talked to police from his hospital bed while suffering from a bullet wound to the head, and the defendant who was stuck in jail for seven days before he confessed. And let's not forget, Fitts argued, one of Albert Dyer's many confessions was before the grand jury, under oath, with, according to Fitts' account, ample warning that he didn't have to testify. But he did, in great detail.

Finally, an argument about Dyer's silence at trial. He never claimed his confessions weren't voluntary. He never repudiated them. He never testified that he didn't know what he was saying. Fitts wrote, "He has never denied that he committed the murders." Someone had underlined the sentence.

With briefs filed, the case retreated into the shadows as the high court began its lengthy review. And over the next few months, many people would grow impatient with the process.

Chairman State Prison Board   *March 29, 1938*

Dear Sir
I do not want to over step the law, but if it would be permissible, I would like to ask when, if ever, is Albert Dyer, the murderer of my two grandchildren, Melba Everett and Madeline of Inglewood, going to be executed? I wonder why he is allowed to live on while the mother of those children is dragging out her existence, thinking

of the two little graves in Forest Lawn Cemetery, where her daughters lie.

I am a broken down old woman but I could help pull the switch that would send him into eternity, after he lured those little girls away from their play and so terribly mutilated their little bodies.

Would you kindly tell me if any progress is made toward his final end? A meaner, more degraded, dirtier skunk never drew breath than he is.

I certainly would appreciate a reply if it would be all right for me to know. Please consider this confidential and should you reply, whatever you tell me will be a sealed book as far as I go.

Thanking you for the favor, I am, a friend of justice.

Rose M. Oliver

THE OTHER PEOPLE calling for swift justice during this time sent their pleas to the governor. Rose Oliver addressed her letter to the prison board and it was forwarded to the warden at San Quentin, so it was tucked away at the State Archives in the prison/execution file.

I went over the documents several times, and I would have seen the reference to her grandchildren, but her letter seemed to just appear one day. I read it carefully. Oliver. My grandmother's maiden name. I got out the family tree and my grandmother's birth certificate, and discovered yet another piece of family history in this old story. Rose May Oliver was my great-grandmother.

ROSE AND OTHERS would not have to wait much longer for the final verdict on Albert Dyer. And no one was very surprised when the California Supreme Court finally issued its decision in late May, affirming Dyer's conviction. Writing for the majority, Justice Curtis Edmonds penned these choice words for the defendant:

> *His story is that of a degenerate fiend. After getting the little girls to leave the park where they were playing on the pretext that he would take them rabbit hunting, he led them to the lonely place in the hills where he carried out his diabolical designs. The entire*

*record clearly shows that there has been no miscarriage of justice;
hence the challenged rulings are not a ground for reversal. There
are a number of inconsistencies in the details of the events related by
the defendant on different occasions, but he repeatedly stated that
he murdered the children. One cannot read the complete statements
which the defendant made without reaching the certain conclusion
that the evidence overwhelmingly supports the jury's verdicts.*

AND ON JUNE 29, 1938, while Dyer languished on the Row at San
Quentin, Superior Court Judge Scott signed an order in his Los
Angeles courtroom. Albert W. Dyer was to be hanged by the neck on
September 16, 1938. A few hours later, the court clerk certified the
official death warrant and sent it to the warden up north.

It was over. And everyone knew it.

Everyone except thousands of people in Southern California.

SAVING ALBERT DYER

Inglewood, California
July 1938

A WEEK AFTER the court's decision, Wright's group, now officially known as the Dyer Case Investigating Committee, chaired by real estate man R. E. Perry, took their fight to save Dyer all the way to the governor's office.

On June 1, attorney Ralph Evans sent the sworn statements he'd taken, and a few days later, State Assembly Speaker William Moseley Jones followed up with his versions. Copies were also delivered to the California Supreme Court.

On June 13, the Municipal League of Los Angeles's Committee on Industrial Relations and Law Enforcement called its members to hear testimony in preparation for urging the governor to spare Dyer. The notice is signed by the League's secretary Morey Stanley Mosk, who went on to be a distinguished and the longest-serving (thirty-seven years) justice on the California Supreme Court. The meeting must have gone well because on July 9, the League wrote to Governor Merriam outlining its own investigation and citing the case's most troubling facts—the lack of fingerprint and blood evidence, the impossible walk, the questionable confessions, and from their own digging, three jurors who were unsure about the verdict. In their letter to the Governor, they urged an exhaustive investigation and closed by respectfully noting that "the only interest the League or its Board has is to avoid an irreparable miscarriage of justice."

On July 18, Inglewood mayor Raymond Darby joined the call for an investigation with his own letter to Governor Merriam. Among other arguments, he said he knew Dyer quite well through his work as a crossing guard:

Of my own knowledge I could say that his mentality is very, very low. Today is a beautiful day. A year ago in May, a day very similar to this, he came to me complaining that WPA officials had taken away their [crossing guards'] rain coats and would I see that they were returned to them.

The fate of Albert Dyer rests in your hands. If he is guilty I am sure that there is only one punishment that befits his case and that is death. If, on the other hand, he is innocent, he should not die but should be cared for in an institution for such as he. If you are unable to make a complete investigation of this between now and September 16th I would suggest to you that you stay the execution as of that date in order that you may go into every phase of this.

The letters kept coming from all over, including a handwritten note from Mrs. Emma Berkley of Inglewood, pleading that Dyer had no car, couldn't drive, and shouldn't that alone be enough Mr. Governor?

In newspaper interviews, Williams from the DA's office branded the statements—the whole thing—"politics" and "worthless." Both his office and the Los Angeles County Sheriff refused to investigate. The case was closed.

A SECOND LOOK

Sacramento, California
July 10–15, 1938

WHILE THE CASE was deemed closed in the Los Angeles District Attorney's office, not so in the governor's office. The governor had the power to grant Dyer a reprieve, so he could effectively negate the death sentence won by the DA's office. Governor Merriam may have been trying to avoid a political firestorm or perhaps he and his staff were genuinely interested in the truth, but either way, they decided to take a second look at the Dyer matter—a look that turned out to be very quick and one-sided.

Governor Merriam assigned the task to the state's Criminal Identification and Investigation Division, part of the California Department of Justice under the state attorney general. The division chief, C. S. Morrill, appointed Harry Hickock, a special criminal investigator, to head the investigation into Dyer's case. In Hickock's report to Morrill, which Morrill then provided to the governor, Hickock said the investigation involved reading the trial transcript and all the affidavits, reviewing the DA's case file, and interviewing public officials and witnesses.

But his report reveals interviews only with the state's primary players, law enforcement and attorneys, all the same men who investigated and prosecuted the case, "all of whom expressed their opinion that Dyer was the right man." DA Buron Fitts even detailed in writing all the reasons Dyer was guilty, including Dyer's damning description of the gate, which was never established at trial or elsewhere. Hickock did not interview anyone from the defense.

Instead of witnesses, he interviewed the doctors who testified at trial and before the grand jury, which was curious because their conclusions were already part of the transcript—and the doctors' responses to Hickock's questioning are a replay of that testimony. And all of them testified for the prosecution, except two who testified for both sides. Not surprisingly, they, too, had no doubt about Dyer's guilt. Dr. Boehme, who testified for the prosecution, clearly supported Dyer's fate. "He would have been better to have been taken out of his existence when he was born. Just a poor miserable wretch."

Hickock did manage to unearth one psychiatrist, Victor Parkin, who examined Dyer for the defense. Parkin expressed serious concerns about Dyer's mental state and the events leading to his confessions. Hickock's stenographer captured Dr. Parkin's sworn statement about his interview with Dyer shortly after Dyer was arrested:

> He [Dyer] told me "I was feared by what the officers said to me." He said "they kept questioning me and threatening to slap me—they got me all feared up and I told them lies about what I had done." He said one of them said "Sit down or I will knock your teeth down your throat, you son-of-a-bitch." When I questioned [Dyer] about the difficulty he said "I did not do it, in my heart God knows I did not do it." I said "What do you mean by saying in your heart you did not do it." His answer was "In my heart, I did not do it." You mean that you are sorry you did it." He said "No, I did not do it, they got me all feared up and I lied to them."

Parkin never testified for either side, saying he couldn't be sure about anything—the physical evidence was inconclusive and "I disregarded the confession—I do not think it means a darn. I have always had my doubt as to his killing the little girls and when I say always, I have never been entirely without a doubt."

AS FOR THE new suspect, Jensen, he was interviewed twice—not under oath, but with a stenographer present. But rather than Hickock interviewing Jensen alone, or utilizing investigators from his own office, he assigned Jack Sumner, an investigator with the Los Angeles County District Attorney's office, to question Jensen. Sumner met with Jensen, along with two investigators/detectives, Captain Winn and Detective McDonnell, also from the DA's office. So, the first and most extensive interview with Jensen was conducted by three representatives of the office that convicted Dyer, two of whom, Sumner and Winn, were involved in investigating and questioning Dyer after he was first arrested. Hickock wasn't even there.

Jensen seemed to have answers for everything—he was mowing lawns that day, just check with his customers; he didn't own a Ford at the time and didn't know how to drive that type of vehicle even if he'd had one. He was candid about his problems with his neighbors, who seemed to have it out for him. And he damaged the credibility of Wright and Perry by recounting how they'd impersonated police officers by coming to Jensen's and his neighbors' homes, flashing badges, and asking questions like they were detectives. They'd told Jensen he was going to walk the thirteen steps to the scaffold for what he'd done to those girls. Someone was always following him.

In his second statement, Jensen sounds like a man on the brink—stalked, accused, investigated, and ruined. Indeed, a couple of weeks earlier, he'd been charged with mayhem. He'd confronted real estate man Perry and allegedly bit his ear. Jensen mentioned those problems in his second interview and denied the ear-biting incident, but investigators stuck to the matter at hand and continued to question him about the Dyer matter.

Investigators also took unsworn statements from Jensen's alleged customers and from the man he said sold him the old Ford. Everyone was trying to remember events from almost a year earlier, so there were a few holes in the details, but for the most part, Jensen's story checked out.

Carl Jensen had seemed a promising suspect with his distinctive voice, the tattoos on his forearms, and the old Ford in his yard, but the investigation yielded no game-changing revelations. Nothing material was surfacing with Jensen either because the wrong people were asking the questions or he really had nothing to do with any of it.

HICKOCK ALSO VISITED Dyer at San Quentin. Dyer denied any involvement, saying he was forced into confessing. But a death row officer told Hickock that three months earlier Dyer confessed to him and asked for a minister, and Dyer apparently did so again later with another officer. Coincidentally, the warden wrote to Public Defender Vercoe on July 10 reporting the same thing, but he'd added that when the prison psychiatrist questioned Dyer after his admissions, he denied everything. Hickock did not report similar findings.

Hickock closed his report about the prison visit with a strange observation—strange that he thought it proved anything. He said he noticed Dyer had tattoos on his forearms, and a man seen with the girls the day they were kidnapped also had arm tattoos. But a lot of men had arm tattoos. Men like Fred Godsey. And Carl Jensen. And so many of the early suspects before Dyer was interrogated and confessed.

In the end, Hickock loosely concluded, "It seems logical to assume that if there are sufficient facts corroborating Albert Dyer's confession to having committed these crimes, then Carl Jensen in all probability had nothing to do with them."

Hickock never interviewed any of the people trying to save Dyer, not Lillian Pop or Amy Lancey, or anybody else who was in the park in June 1937.

He spent just five days on the case. Six, if you count his visit to San Quentin.

ON AUGUST 22, Perry sent the Governor a Petition for Clemency signed by several thousand Californians. A week later he followed up with the official Application for Executive Clemency with a statement from Dyer:

I think I should have a pardon because I know I have never done any crime because plead not guilty I am a innocent man. Of those three little children.

IT'S NOT SURPRISING that a toothless investigation kept Dyer on track for the gallows. Upsetting the apple cart of a final conviction is nearly impossible even in the best cases. A jury verdict of guilty is presumed, legally and philosophically, to be the final word, beyond reproach. We correctly allow appeals and other reviews, but litigation can't be endless—legally, financially, and otherwise—so those remedies are legitimately limited by time and procedural rules. But those logistics aside, our criminal justice system and we ourselves so value the finality of judgments that we almost always err on the side of leaving things alone. And in the case of wrongful convictions, where we are working to expose errors made in police stations, courtrooms, laboratories, and execution chambers, we are often rolling the boulder up a steep and densely-hurdled hill. The exoneration annals are filled with examples.

Like the Michael Morton case in Texas, in which private and Innocence Project attorneys fought for five years to perform DNA testing on a key piece of evidence that could help exonerate him—five more years that Morton spent in prison, five years added to the twenty he'd already served for a crime he didn't commit. His case also revealed serious prosecutorial misconduct; so serious, it led to the first ever criminal investigation and conviction of a prosecutor for acts committed in their professional capacity. The state fought every effort to investigate Morton's case, all at taxpayer expense and all in the name of preserving justice.

And in a more extreme expression of this mind-set, the late Justice Antonin Scalia of the US Supreme Court wrote in 2009 in the case of death row inmate Troy Davis: "This Court has never held that the Constitution forbids the execution of a convicted defendant who has had a full and fair trial but is later able to convince a habeas court that he is 'actually' innocent." Scalia's conclusion was technically correct—the court has not ruled on the discrete issue—but his conclusion is a reminder that the practice of executing innocents is still acceptable in some camps, and attorneys have argued for execution in other cases on similar grounds.

The reluctance to disturb convictions is also evidenced by how difficult it can be to access evidence for forensic testing. In approximately 43 percent of cases, DNA testing helps us find the real perpetrator, so it's in everyone's interest to get to the truth. But the truth is often inconvenient, and obstacles are still numerous and challenging. All fifty states now allow some access, but laws vary and the legal gauntlet can be brutal and expensive, in large part, to preserve the finality of convictions. On the upside, twelve states have formed "innocence commissions" to investigate prior cases that may have resulted in wrongful convictions.

But preserving finality remains a top priority for many and arguably the most compelling reason is concern for the victims. When we question convictions, we open old wounds, forcing victims and families to relive everything, and in many cases, to fear the release of someone they believe is guilty. Most exoneration cases raise this concern and it can be one of the most challenging forces to overcome. It certainly has been for me, wondering how my family would feel— how I really feel—about my concerns for Dyer. The two are difficult to reconcile. When we identify at all with the convicted, we must be betraying the victims.

But the newspapers were silent about my grandparents and the Stephens family—no stories about how they felt about their tight-knit community and beyond supporting Albert Dyer, keeping their nightmare alive.

Maybe nothing mattered anymore, or maybe they focused on the positive. I've often looked for clues in my family's life after June 1937, and surprisingly, they stayed in Inglewood. Shortly after the murders, they moved away from Hazel Street, but not far. Then after my grandfather died, my grandmother moved to a smaller house, still in Inglewood, near the park and the Baldwin Hills. For some reason, she lived much of her remaining life there, with all those landmarks of pain. She seemed to live a relatively happy life though, working as a bookkeeper, staying active in her church, and spoiling her grand-children. But I can never quite shake my great-grandmother's letter saying how my grandmother was "dragging out her existence."

My grandparents may have been fully convinced about Dyer, or maybe their doubts lingered as time ticked away on Death Row, but either way, it must have been incredibly painful during the summer of 1938, suspended in time like that, waiting for something—a reprieve or a hanging.

THE TELEGRAMS

Sacramento, California
September 1938

EARNESTLY REQUEST REPRIEVE IN EXECUTION OF ALBERT
DYER PENDING INVESTIGATION HIS INNOCENCE. VOLUMINOUS
EVIDENCE AND AFFIDAVITS INDICATE POSSIBLE MISCARRIAGE
OF JUSTICE=
   JACK B TENNEY ASSEMBLYMAN 46TH DISTRICT

THE DATE SET FOR THE EXECUTION OF ALBERT DYER IS VERY
NEAR STOP WE HAVE NOT HEARD FROM YOU THE RESULT
OF THE SPECIAL INVESTIGATION WHICH YOU PROMISED INTO
AFFIDAVITS SUBMITTED STOP MAY WE HAVE THE COURTSTY
OF A REPORT=
   ANTHONY PRATT SECRETARY MUNICIPAL LEAGUE OF LOS
   ANGELES

URGENTLY REQUEST YOU REPRIEVE ALBERT DYER EVIDENCE
IN YOUR POSSESSION PROOF OF GROSS MISCARRIAGE OF
JUSTICE=
   HASKELL P WRIGHT.

THOUSANDS DOUBT ALBERT DYER'S GUILT STOP REPRIEVE
PENDING INVESTIGATION APPEARS JUSTIFIED=
   ROBERT H BLACK LOS ANGELES TOWN MEETING.

CERTAIN ALBERT DYER INNOCENT PARK SUPERVISOR WRIGHT
R E PERRY & OTHERS SAW SAILOR EDDIE WITH CHILDREN.
ANYONE WOULD SAY YES TO EVERY THING A HARD THIRD
DEGREE COULD SAY MORE THANKS FOR YOUR GOOD DEEDS
YOU HAVE BEEN A VERY GOOD GOVERNOR
    MRS E F MCGINESS.

IN REGISTERED MAIL TODAY LETTER REGARDING ALBERT
DIER CASE. PLEASE RUSH READING SAME CAREFULLY
BEFORE TIME SET FOR EXECUTION OF HIM AND IF POSSIBLE
GRANT CHANGE OF SENTENCE TO IMPRISONMENT=
EMRY B LACY.

LATE ON SEPTEMBER 15, 1938, while telegrams, letters, and phone calls flooded the governor's office, guards moved Dyer from San Quentin's Condemned Row to the Death House, a room just off the execution chamber, where he would spend his last night. None of the men on death row said good-bye or anything else as Dyer walked down the corridor, past the Row and "Siberia," and beyond to the Death House. Most didn't even look at him. He would not be missed. *Good riddance, you cowardly child killer. Good riddance, Albert the Chickenhearted.*

THE TAINTED JUROR

Inglewood, California
September 15, 1938

JUROR HAROLD HARBY cried foul at the last possible moment. In a written statement provided to defense attorneys the day before Dyer's execution, which the attorneys quickly telegrammed to the governor, Harby wrote:

> *I did not believe then, and I do not believe now, that Albert Dyer is guilty.*

He admitted that he was the lone holdout when the Dyer jury was deadlocked 11 to 1 for two days during deliberations, and that other jurors subjected him to "harassment and constant verbal abuse, including his roommate at the Rosslyn hotel who moved out the last night saying he 'would be damned if he would stay in the room with a skunk'" like Harby.

That same night Bailiff Putney told Harby that Judge White believed Dyer was "guilty as hell." Harby asked to see Judge White, but the bailiff said it was not allowed. Harby decided the judge must have more information than the jurors did so he would have to vote for conviction and he did, "although in my heart I felt I was still doing wrong." He claimed that he held out for life imprisonment instead of the death penalty, but lost that battle as well.

Apparently feeling guilty watching the clock run down on Albert Dyer's life, Harby contacted Judge White the day before on September 14 and told him the story. Judge White told Harby he had never expressed an opinion about the case until the trial was over and the verdict was returned. Harby concluded that someone lied to him about the judge's opinion and that his vote was the result of undue influence.

> *This statement is taken at my insistence because I know the hours are short in which I can do something to undo the wrong that I did to Albert Dyer.*

Attorneys Neeley and Cuff told the press they had forwarded Harby's statement to the governor via telephone, telegram, and air mail, and requested a reprieve. But at 10:00 that night, about the time Dyer was moved to the Death House at San Quentin, the governor's office indicated that he had received no such communication.

So, Harby sent his own telegram the morning of the execution:

I WAS UNDULY INFLUENCED IN REACHING MY VERDICT ON DYER. THEREFOR CASE SHOULD BE DECLARED MISTRIAL. YOU HAVE 4000 SIGNATURES REQUESTING STAY OF EXECUTION. VARIOUS AFFIDAVITS IN YOUR HANDS DIRECTLY LINK ANOTHER MAN WITH THE INGLEWOOD MURDER CASE COULD YOU EVER SLEEP IN PEACE IF YOU NOW REFUSE THE STAY OF EXECUTION WHEN THERE IS SO MUCH EVIDENCE SINCE THE TRIAL POINTING TO ANOTHER AS GUILTY FIEND PLEASE WIRE ME YOUR DECISION. I AM SO VITALLY CONCERNED =
   HAROLD HARBY

BUT THE GOVERNOR was not persuaded by any of it. In his official statement to the press early on Dyer's execution date, he concluded that "nothing has been presented to me which in any way indicates the innocence of Albert Dyer. On the contrary, an examination of the trial transcript and the 160-page report of Harry C. Hickok, investigator of the State Bureau of Criminal Identification and Investigation, which discloses sufficient facts to corroborate the many confessions made by Albert Dyer before different persons, including several reputable physicians under many different circumstances, justifies the refusal to extend clemency."

THE LONG DROP

San Quentin State Prison, San Quentin, California
September 16, 1938

AT 3 A.M. on September 16, 1938, a carrier pigeon flew through an open window into San Quentin's execution chamber and landed in the rafters high above the gallows.

At 5:30 a.m., Dyer rose and ordered the traditional breakfast for the condemned: ham and eggs, hotcakes and coffee.

At 7 a.m., the prison hangman checked the gallows one last time. He'd set up the rope for a "long drop" because Dyer was so small. The hangman needed to get a clean break of the neck without beheading the prisoner and the long drop was the only way to do that with someone so light. He checked and rechecked his calculations. Around him, prison staff were trying everything to catch the pigeon, but it fluttered from lofty perch to perch, always just out of reach.

At 9:45 a.m., Reverend Thomas Gale, a San Francisco Baptist minister, and A. C. Schmitt, the prison chaplain, joined Dyer in the anteroom.

At 10:00, Warden Court Smith came for Dyer.

Dyer pleaded with the ministers, "Please write two letters for me saying good-bye—one to my foster mother in Redondo Beach and another to my real mother living at Indian Lake, New York. And please make them stop persecuting my wife. They should not have sent her to the feeble-minded home. She is a good woman."

"All right, Dyer, we have to go now," the warden ordered.

"Give me a last cigarette please."

A guard put the cigarette in Dyer's mouth and lit it for him. Dyer pulled on the cigarette and then held it in his left hand. He never took another drag because guards quickly strapped his arms to his sides for the walk to the gallows.

Fifty-four spectators, including Don Oliver, my grandmother's brother from the LAPD, watched his last walk down the stairs from the death house and into the chamber, past the crowd to the base of the gallows. Some noticed the mysterious pigeon, head cocked to the side, blinking curiously down on the procession.

Then thirteen steps up. The black hood and then the noose. A guard removed the cigarette from Dyer's left hand.

And at 10:03, the two hangmen pulled their respective levers, neither knowing which one had opened the door beneath Dyer. The trap banged open and he dropped through. The long rope jerked tight at the bottom. The hangman got his nice clean break.

Don Oliver turned to another spectator and said, "He's getting what he deserved."

Thirteen minutes later the prison physician pronounced Dyer dead and the hangman's assistants cut down his body.

The pigeon took flight and a few prison staffers moved toward the gallows to get up high enough to catch it. But within seconds, it was gone, out the open window it flew in earlier that morning.

ALBERT DYER CONTINUED to make news even in death. The *Los Angeles Times* ran the story of his execution on page one, front and center, right next to a piece about the growing problems in Europe with a German fascist named Adolf Hitler.

But the *Los Angeles Times* headline was the only memorial of Dyer's passing. His foster mother, Etta Young, couldn't afford to claim his body and he was buried in the old San Quentin Boot Hill cemetery with a wooden stake at the head of the grave carved with his inmate number: 60804. He was thirty-three years old.

THE FIGHT FOR Albert Dyer ended on September 16 at San Quentin, but the questions remain—questions about his guilt or innocence, and questions about his punishment.

It's difficult to close the book on his story when considering the hundreds of cases in which defendants who have appeared so apparently guilty turn out to be actually innocent, not exonerated on a legal technicality but proven innocent through DNA evidence, which evidence often leads to the real killer or rapist.

The errors are always disturbing, caused by the same issues in Dyer's case: problematic eyewitness identifications, questionable confessions, faulty—or no—physical evidence, and a district attorney's office zealous to win justice for innocent victims. The logistics in these cases are challenging enough, but introduce the possibility of human error inherent in our jury system, especially in a case where the bar for conviction is low because of the collective demand for justice, and we have the recipe for these too-frequent miscarriages of justice—and reason to continue questioning convictions like Dyer's.

Fortunately, through years of tireless work by the Innocence Project and other organizations like it, reforms in law enforcement and scientific practices are reducing risks on the front end of the criminal justice process, and lawyers and judges are using evolving procedural laws to keep many of the errors in check at trial. Further, an increasing willingness to recognize past errors is allowing us to exonerate innocents, many in the nick of time. Since 1973 in the United States, 156 people awaiting execution on death row have been exonerated.

But Dyer's case is a reminder that there is no chance to right these wrongs when the deed is done.

Perhaps he put it best when he said, "This is a terrible thing for an innocent man to have to face. The right man will come along some day and really confess to those crimes after I'm dead and gone and then it will be too late to save me."

AFTERWORD

MY JOURNEY IS over and I wish it wasn't. While the process of learning about my family's tragedy was painful, it's also made me feel like I was with them—in the little house on Hazel Street with my grandparents and aunt and uncle, on their front porch across from the park, at the kitchen table with my dad and grandma, penning a letter with my unexpected and spirited great-grandmother. They are all more fully in my heart now, but I will miss spending my days with them. I will especially miss being close to the memories of those two little girls who have given me the greatest gifts, of family and history and understanding.

Sadly, memories—a few stories and photographs—are all I have, and probably will ever have because my family and others buried this story away so deeply. I felt that effect acutely when I interviewed my dad's third wife, Adrienne, with whom he was so close and so in love for many years, feeling certain he'd shared the story with her. She replied, "What sisters?" I can't imagine him keeping anything from Adrienne, but in eleven years of marriage, he'd never even mentioned them. Olive was the only sister Adrienne knew about.

So, the little bit of information I did find is so precious to me.

In 2007, in its online Daily Mirror feature about Los Angeles history, the *Los Angeles Times* published a piece about the case with reflections from Theresa Pinamonti-Ziegler, who was seven years old in 1937. I tracked her down and we made our first contact by email in 2011. I explained who I was and wondered if she remembered my aunts. She replied right away:

> Hi Pamela,
> I got the chills when I read your email. I am so sorry that you missed out on knowing your aunties. I only played with them that one day and they were such sunny, bright and happy little girls. So innocent. It was something that affected me all my life and at 81, can still see those little girls and I playing there at Centinela park. We were right next to a big pipe of some sort that was big enough for us to run in and out of and I can still hear the peals of laughter in our voices.

We emailed and talked by phone several times, and she helped me form a wonderful new image in my mind, with smiles and laughter at play on a beautiful summer day. And Howard Hilborn gave me similar gifts of memory. I found his name in the comments to another online feature about the case and we connected by phone. I was so touched hearing him remember with such clarity how Marie dazzled her elementary school classmates with her song.

But these and a few other details are the only links to my aunts, and perhaps my story will help others realize that, no matter how painful, we should share these histories so victims are not lost and so future generations can know all that came before them and what molded their parents, grandparents, and others. And even in the darkest histories, there can be joys to discover. In my case, learning about my aunts' deaths has brought them to life for me, Marie singing to her class, little Madeline hugging the trunk of their favorite pepper tree at the park, the two of them skipping to school, hand in hand, smiling and laughing. And because I've learned about all of it, the darkness and the light, I'm enriched, walking through my days with a deeper sense of past, my family and their stories a real part of me. What an unexpected gift when all I wanted was to memorialize two little girls who were almost erased forever.

IN 2015, I visited their graves at Forest Lawn in Glendale. The old Graceland section was down a narrow road that wound through grassy hills and valleys, giant stately old trees and beautiful banks of azalea. As I approached the end of the road, there on the left, I immediately recognized the hill from the photographs of the funeral, the one where my grandparents stood nearly eighty years earlier. I climbed the hill and found the little bronze tablets, side by side. Marie and Madeline.

I knelt down, then sat down, and spent time there. If such sacred places are a connection to those we've lost, then maybe they heard my whispers—*I'm so sorry, I wish I'd known you. You are not forgotten. You are forever in my heart.*

It was hard to leave them. I put their pictures in a small heart-shaped frame and left it at the graves, so I could turn back as I made my way down that now-familiar hill and say good-bye to their smiling faces. And that's how I'll remember them—no longer forgotten, no longer mere footnotes to Albert Dyer's fading narrative. Forever young, their hair soft and angelic in the California sunshine, their hearts bursting with love and hopeful tomorrows.

ACKNOWLEDGMENTS

THE AUTHOR WISHES to thank the following people for all their help in making this book possible:

Larry Harnisch of the Los Angeles Times; Christina Rice, Senior Librarian of the photo collection at the Los Angeles Public Library; Ryan Brubacher, Prints & Photographs Reference Librarian at the Library of Congress; Jill Jokisch at Getty Images; Leslie Stauffer, Research Editor at Getty Images; Erica Varela of the *Los Angeles Times*; Molly Haigh with the Charles E. Young Research Library Special Collections at UCLA; the devoted stewards of history at the California State Archives; June Hazley-Quimby; Howard Hilborn; Theresa Pinamonte-Ziegler; Olga Greco; my agent Carol Mann and her staff, in particular Lydia (Blyfield) Shamah and Eliza Dreier; Mark Gompertz, Caroline Russomanno, Brian Peterson, Leslie Davis and everyone at Skyhorse Publishing; my sister Christine Schwab for connecting me with Carol Mann and for endless enthusiasm about my story; my sister Madlynne Peterson for sharing her own research and invaluable family stories; my sister Susan Whittaker for reading one of those early under-baked drafts and supporting the book anyway; Kimberlee Orenstein for the magic of October 2016 when Skyhorse said yes, and so much more; Nancy Donahue for nearly a decade of unwavering and infectious faith; the selfless heroes at the Innocence Project, the California Innocence Project, and the many other organizations of people dedicated to exonerating the wrongfully convicted; and Earl Shidler, the best friend in all the world.

NOTES

FOR MORE INFORMATION and inspiration on wrongful convictions, I recommend the following excellent works: *Actual Innocence*, Barry Scheck, Peter Neufeld and Jim Dwyer (New American Library, 2000); *Journey Toward Justice*, Dennis Fritz (Seven Locks Press, 2006); *Exit to Freedom*, Calvin C. Johnson, Jr. with Greg Hampikian (University of Georgia Press, 2003); *Picking Cotton*, Jennifer Thompson-Cannino, Ronald Cotton & Erin Torneo (St. Martin's Press, 2009); *Killing Time*, John Holloway and Ronald M. Gauthier (Skyhorse Publishing, 2010); *The Central Park Five*, Sarah Burns (Knopf, 2011); *Convicting the Innocent*, Brandon Garrett (Harvard University Press, 2011) and *Anatomy of Innocence: Testimonies of the Wrongfully Convicted*, Caldwell & Klinger (Liveright, 2017). *See also* www.innocenceproject.org, www.californiainnocenceproject.org, and www.law.northwestern.edu./cwc/.